SIMPLY MINIMAL

SIMPLY MINIMAL

Your Guide to a Stress-Free Life

KATELYN CRESMER

CHRISTEAH PRESS
CHAMBERSBURG, PA
2018

CHRISTEAH

CHRISTEAH Press

Chambersburg, PA

ISBN: 978-1-7322631-0-9
Library of Congress Control Number: 2018909183

BOOK DESIGN BY KATELYN CRESMER
PHOTOGRAPHS BY KATELYN CRESMER

GET A **FREE** 7-DAY MINI-DECLUTTERING COURSE

Get a jump-start on decluttering in one week with a small decuttering mission each day. Plus, get a coupon code for 10% off the ebook version of Simply Minimal.

Head on over to greenasathistle.com/hello

This one is for Mamie.

Simple settings
Lovely land.
It's how I want to live my life.

In reality,
There's no fantasy
And everything is depressed.

In this small time
In my life
I'm dying
And all I want is
Simple settings
Lovely land.

I might be
Dead before
I get it in the end.

I'll be happy.
But for right now,
Simple settings
Lovely land
Is years
Away.

contents

Visualize

an american dreams

Our culture is being run by marketing plots, greed and habits. Ads now follow you around the internet bullying you into buying objects. Companies are enticing you with poorly made products that you don't need and will never use to make a buck. You are in a cycle of trying to make money so you can spend it on objects to impress society or achieve the "American Dream."

The "American Dream" is a goal society embedded into our minds to make us work hard towards something, sometimes unattainable, or it will make us feel left out or a failure when we don't achieve it. We must have a college education, a big house, several cars, a marriage and kids. Not to mentions the "decorations" such as a pool, hot tub, vacation house, garden, huge garage and a couple of pets.

These are great if you truly want them and truly value them, but they are designed to put a hold on your money, throw you into debt and keep you working jobs that suck the life out of you just to keep paying for the dream.

An average education costs $80,000. A huge house costs $300,000. A car costs $25,000. A wedding costs $26,000. To raise a child today costs $233,000. A hot tub costs $5,000. And let's not forget to mention all the money we put out to buy all the stuff for our homes and the clothes for our family because once you obtain the pieces of the dream, the expenses are not over. You have to pay for maintenance. You have to pay for objects to fill the spaces. And you have to pay for renovations and upgrades because you won't be happy with the objects for long.

You thought the "American Dream" would make you happy. That's what society says! But, the glamour will wear off and maybe a new kitchen or car will satisfy you. Soon you'll realize that this dream is a trap to keep you in debt so you have to keep working to pay off the debt.

Why are we putting ourselves through this? Is

this really what you want? Have you ever thought about if you ever wanted a house or a mortgage? Do you want several cars or a pool? These things are nice, but they won't make you happy. They just add stress, bills and labor.

There's another way to enjoy items. You can have everything you need and be happy. There's this philosophy called minimalism. Minimalism, as defined by Joshua Becker from becomingminimalist.com, is the intentional promotion of the things we most value and the removal of everything that distracts us from it. This idea allows us to live a simple and happy life.

In simple terms: get rid of everything unimportant from your life and keep everything that is essential, that serves you and that you truly love.

So if you only own what you truly need and enjoy and give up the rest, you will feel better and your life will improve. And wait... There's more! Minimalism doesn't stop at your stuff. It can be applied to every area of your life to better your life from every angle.

You can better your health, finances, relationships and personal growth.

It takes time, but you can make the life you've been dying to have without working until 65. Your life can be blissful, simple. All you have to do is minimize everything unimportant.

And that's what this book is about. Showing you tips and road maps you can apply to your journey. I want this book to be a reference book in case you get stuck. In case you don't know how to move forward.

Before we get started, let's learn more about minimalism and how great it is.

What it Means to be a Minimalist

Being a minimalist means living a minimalist life-style and practicing minimalism. Every item you own, everything you buy, every choice you make is meant to bring you closer to a life of meaning. Living a meaningful life is one goal of a minimalist.

Leo Babauta says it's living without an obsession with material things or an obsession with doing everything and doing too much. It's using simple tools, having a simple wardrobe, carrying little and living lightly.

It does not mean you have to live without, that you can't have things or that you have to restrict your life. It simply means every area of your life is purposeful and deliberate to make your life the best it can be.

Benefits of Living Simply

By becoming a minimalist and reducing all of the unnecessary things in your life, you will receive nothing but positive benefits. If you add minimalism in your life, your life will be filled with good and positivity. Everything you care about and everything that makes you joyous will be front and center in your life. Everything you dislike and everything that makes you upset, mad or angry can be greatly reduced.

There are so many benefits to minimalism. There's a crazy thing that happens when you have less in your life – you gain so many things. You'll experience less of the negative stuff like clutter and stress, and you'll experience more of the positive stuff like time and freedom. Here are the benefits of minimalism:

less worry

Worry comes from a feeling of overwhelm. Owning less and ridding your life of unnecessary objects, commitments, bad relationships, money problems and stress, frees your mind from those things.

Worry will go away. Not permanently – you will

still worry about your family, if someone isn't doing well or if your children are safe – but worries about debt, time, social commitments, work and health will all come to an end.

less clutter

You were probably brought to this book on a thought of a clutter-free life. Minimalism will help you achieve this. You will never have to spend an entire day doing housework again. You won't have to organize anymore and everything you own will serve a purpose in your life.

less cleaning

Owning fewer things makes cleaning so much easier. When your living area is filled with stuff, you have more things to clean. Things get dusty; you have to clean. Things get unorganized; you have to clean. Random items end up on the floor; you have to clean. But, if you had less stuff, you wouldn't have to keep organizing and reorganizing. You wouldn't have to clean as much, thus saving you time and stress.

Some chores, such as dishes and laundry, are a big stress inducer especially when you have too many dishes and clothes. Have you ever went to the sink with every single dish stuffed in it because someone was too lazy to wash the dishes they used and ended up reaching for a clean dish instead?

Same thing with laundry. We tend to wear all our clean clothes before washing them making laundry day an all-day affair. Or some of us just wear a fraction of our clothes and never touch the ones in the back of the closet and those clothes just end up taking space away from you. But, with less, dishes become a breeze and laundry becomes a weekly load or two.

less dread

Dread will go away when everything you are doing is giving you meaning and purpose. You don't dread things you want to do; you anticipate them!

more money

If you're wishing for more money, minimalism is the way to go. By buying only what we need, we save what we used to spend frivolously. By simplifying our lives, money becomes easier to manage, easier to hold onto and easier to be put to uses that make us happy such as traveling, hobbies and self-development.

Some people even make money by becoming a minimalist. By selling the things you don't use anymore, you can gain quick profits that you otherwise would not have had. But, it doesn't stop there. You'll see all the unnecessary bills you could live without. Subscription services, cable, phone services, internet, rent and utilities are all bills that could be reduced or canceled.

By gaining more time, you could also start making more money from the things you love to do. Many people start side businesses with their hobbies. Minimalism helps them gain the time and focus that they need to do this.

more freedom

Utilizing your time gives you the ability to do the things you want to do. You'll gain the freedom in making choices that benefit you – that you want to do.

more portable

Being portable means being mobile; not grounded. You're not tied down. You can move freely about your life however you want. If you want to move across the country, nothing is stopping you. Nothing is tying you down. Your possessions will not weigh you down.

more time

Time is a gift that we all have so little of. We should make every moment count. Minimalism allows us to have more time by simplifying our lives. When we reduce our time cleaning, worrying, watching TV, dealing with bad relationships and attending social activities, we gain more time to be put towards other things. Have you ever felt that there isn't enough time in a day? Are you so caught up on chores, commitments and work that you don't have time for yourself or your health?

It will feel so nice to finally have time to spare. To have nothing to worry about. You can finally allow yourself to get caught up in the moment, to watch the sunset, to dream.

better health

By simplifying our lives, our health receives many benefits. By reducing our time commitments, busyness, cleaning and debt, our stress will lessen. By getting time back, we'll be able to focus on getting healthy. We can simplify our diets and exercises, so you get just enough and nothing less. You can spend time cooking, time at the gym and less time being stressed about life.

You'll see a major shift in your mood, your happiness levels will go up and you'll feel more vibrant. Stress leads to a lot of health disadvantages.

These benefits are yours for the taking. By applying the tips in this book to your life, you will live life with a different mindset. Life won't be perfect. I can't promise perfection because there are some areas of life that you will dislike and you cannot get rid of things such as school (for minors), work, politics and world tragedies. But, you can put a deliberate step forward and change your life for the better.

Examples of Thriving Minimalists

There are many minimalists in varying degrees thriving in their simplified lives. Anyone can be a minimalist. College students, single mothers, whole families, travelers, me and even you. I would like to highlight a few minimalists with different situations, so you can see their energies and how their lives have gotten so much better since they have simplified. I will share with you a brief highlight of what makes them unique and give you a link to their website if you want to read more about them.

No Impact Man

Colin Beaven did a year-long experiment where he and his family became as green as possible in New York City. They created no trash and they didn't travel if the only way to get to their destination would be to produce carbon. Some would say this is extreme living, but he says that the way most people are living now is extreme.

As he overcame hurdles during his year of no impact, he realized that his old lifestyle and the lifestyles of most people today are extremely wasteful.

Check him out on his website colinbeavan.com. There you can find his book and documentary on his experiment.

Tammy Strobel

Tammy is known for her tiny house. Tiny houses are popular with minimalists because you can live in a tiny space, you can reduce your carbon footprint and you won't be overburdened with clutter in a tiny home.

Everything in the home is deliberate and intentional. Tammy and her husband, Logan, built their tiny house to be functional, cozy and to have plenty of storage. You can see more about her tiny house on

rowdykittens.com.

Leo Babauta

Leo is an author of Zen Habits where he writes about simplicity, minimalism, mindfulness and changing your habits. He is an example of being a minimalist with a family. He and his wife have six children and they all live a very minimal lifestyle together.

He used minimalism, simplifying and meditation to change his bad habits such as smoking, eating junk food and being very sedentary to live a more freeing life where he is healthier, his own boss and happier.

You can read more about Leo on his blog at zenhabits.com.

Minimal Student

Jessica Dang is the author of Minimal Student, a blog, where she documents her journey into minimalism and how she used simplifying her life to travel and find meaning.

She quit her job, packed up a suitcase and went for it! She is a twenty-something nomad who is working on her bucket list that includes running a marathon, getting a black-belt in karate, exploring Hong Kong and Vietnam and learning how to solve a Rubik's cube. Most of her list is already crossed off!

Read more about her at minimalstudent.com.

Colin Wright

Colin Wright is a nomad. He has been homeless for 5 years traveling to a different city every three months. But, it's intentional. Colin runs a blog and his readers are the one who decides where he goes next. He doesn't have a permanent home. All he has is two bags that hold all his possessions.

Colin writes books, runs a blog and runs a publishing company with The Minimalists.

Check him out on exilelifestyle.com

Tannyraw

Tanya is a popular YouTuber who shares with the world how to be a low-fat raw vegan.

Not only is Tanya's diet minimalist, but her life looks minimalist as well. In several videos, she states that she doesn't keep what she doesn't use and that her kitchen drawers must be clutter free.

This woman is a single mother of two kids. Her oldest is not living with her, but she is raising a teenage son by herself. Yet, you can see the vibrancy of her life. Her attitude is so contagious, you'll want to keep watching her videos for her pep talks and motivation

Check out her website at tannyraw.com.

Timothy Ward

Tim is another popular YouTuber who travels all over to work seasonal jobs. He prefers seasonal jobs to a regular, stable job because it gives him a chance to travel, work out in nature and the flexibility to live his minimalist lifestyle without being held down by a permanent residence.

Working seasonal jobs lets him work in the nation's most gorgeous parks. His YouTube channel is filled with inspiration about living with what you need and getting rid of the rest of the things that are holding you back. Search him on YouTube or check out his Twitter:

twitter.com/timothyjward

Becoming Minimalist

Joshua Becker discovered minimalism one day when he was doing the yearly cleaning of his garage. His neighbor came out and proclaimed that her daughter was a minimalist and told her that she didn't need all that stuff. A light bulb went off in Joshua's head and he immediately wanted to know more.

Joshua is a husband and father of two. He decluttered his home, changed his mindset and leads a community on his website becomingminimalist.com.

The Minimalists

Since you've gotten this far in the minimalist world, you may have heard of the Minimalists. These two gentlemen in their early thirties left their 6-figure, corporate jobs to live a simpler life. Since then, they have grown happier, freer and have become debt free.

They are celebrities in the minimalism world with their story, their packing party challenge and their tours, books and documentary. The packing party consists of packing up your home as if you were moving and for a whole month, only unpack what you need in the moment. In the end, after realizing you don't use that much stuff, go through the rest of your things and get rid of things you don't need.

You can see their journey on their website: theminimalists.com.

My Story

I've always loved things. Gadgets, books, stationery, office supplies, journals, etc. Whenever I got something, I would hoard it. I had so many stuffed animals, I sometimes made my room into a zoo and gave my sister a map as she explored it. I had so many unopened stationary supplies that I would keep for years because I didn't want to mess it up or use all of it.

Fast forward to when I'm 19. In that lifespan, my family had moved 15 times. And, somehow I'm always the one with the most boxes. In 2012, we moved to Pittsburgh so I could go to college. We ran out of bedrooms, so I decided to make the attic my room. Technically, it could've been two rooms. My things filled it. But, here's the thing. I was never up there. It was too creepy to sleep up there and the house was so old that the attic was super dusty. I couldn't breathe properly.

Before we moved there, I started fantasizing about living in an RV. I have about 200 bookmarks on RV living, people living in RVs and research on RVs. I guess that planted a seed in my mind because back at the house, and during my last year of college, I literally never went up into my attic room. I slept on the living room couch, with my clothes in an extra fridge that wasn't being used. I kept my hygiene products in the bathroom and my college book bag and that's how I lived. I was always at college or sleeping on the couch.

My fiancé moved in with us Jan. 2014. He brought over all of the things that he needed, and it was literally a few boxes. I started to become somewhat embarrassed at the mess upstairs. So, I started googling simple living and how to get rid of things. I knew that I didn't want this stuff, but the "emotional attachment" I had with things was unbearable at the time.

My family decided we were moving (again), so I thought it was the perfect time to get rid of things, despite having to finish college and complete an internship. Luckily, work at my internship was pretty slow. Because I used that time to research simple living. The first blog about minimalism that I found was Joshua Becker's blog, Becoming Minimalist. I was so enticed that I went to the archives and read every single post in order for a week. This is what I was looking for.

After binge reading 6 years worth of blog posts, I started tackling my attic. I started with the piles and piles of clothes that had found their way to me over the years. Then my sneaker collection which held every sneaker I had since fourth grade. They all still fit me too but were worn down. Then, I made a headway through all the textbooks I had. Then my files. I'm embarrassed to say that I kept every single homework assignment, class note and worksheet since 5th grade. I got rid of a lot, but kept a bunch "for reference."

After the move is when I started my blog, Taking it Back a Notch, to chronicle my journey. I still had a lot of things and boxes. My end goal was to travel and I couldn't travel with all these things weighing me down. I had to get down to business.

So, as I was unpacking at the new place, I started going through each box and repacking what I was officially done with. I started hauling box after box out of my room and to the Goodwill. More clothes, paper, items, decorations and childhood trinkets went away. I remember coming home from my internship and slowly working on my files. Piece by piece; paper by paper. And even though I had the end goal in sight, I was still holding back.

By the time my fiance and I moved into our own place, we had 3 van loads of stuff including furniture. My mom helped us out with her Dodge Caravan and my fiance had his small Hyundai Accent. Using both vehicles, it took three trips. I wanted it to be easier. To be smoother. But, I was making progress, and I was starting to have less stuff than my fiance! The thing is that I was holding back. As I was going through the files, I would have a "reference" folder. I had papers that I wanted to make blog posts out of. It was a struggle.

We moved into a tiny, 415 sq. ft. apartment and it was crowded with our stuff. I didn't want anything else, but we actually needed things. Apparently, when you move out on your own, you need bathroom items such as a plunger, a toilet scrubbing thing and laundry detergent. We also had to get a mop and broom, and while we were at it, we decided to get bar stools and a chair bed. We also had family donate a lot of things including dishes, a microwave, a vacuum and a queen size bed to upgrade from our twin size (talk about being crowded).

We were stuffed and I knew in order to live comfortably, we would have to get rid of things. So, I challenged myself. All throughout 2015, I made videos showing myself decluttering a different area of my apartment complimented with a blog post to hold me accountable. I went through my bookshelf which was like a vertical, catch-all basket. My clothes and my fiance's clothes were sorted through. I went through the bathroom, my chest and then I started going through things again.

I found that decluttering and really decluttering in a minimalist way, is a multi-process. You have to go through your items in rounds. The first round, you are inspired and you go through ruthlessly and you get rid of a big percentage than what you started with. But, there were a lot of "just in case," "maybe, "one day," and "this was a lot of money/a gift/very sentimental" items. And that's what the second round is for. During the second round, you go through the items with a fine-tooth comb and really think about the items. You'll decide to get rid of more things, but leave items that you want to learn to enjoy behind.

After this round, you're still not happy so you make a third. I feel that the process is ongoing until your happy with it. Until you get relief throughout your mind. I believe that it's easier to get rid of items in another round that it was in the first round because you gave your mind some time to process the memories, hopes and values of the object. It needed some time to make a decision.

At the start of me writing this book, I was at the end of my challenge. I've already decluttered all the areas I could find and all that's left is my pictures and my digital clutter. I feel that I'm at a good place with where I'm at, but I still feel that I will continue to downsize until I reach my goals of living in an RV with everything I truly need. But, for right now, I'm good.

Are you good? There's a reason you're reading this. All these changes have impacted other areas of my life from my relationships, commitments and workload to my finances, health and personal growth. I have freed up more time, have become less stressed than ever, have improved finances and have free time for personal growth.

I think it's time to get started on telling you how you can be a minimalist too.

What You Need to be a Minimalist

Here is what you need to become a minimalist:

- an open mind
- willingness to let go or at least a willingness to learn to let go
- strength to work for what you want even if it seems hard

Visualize Your Life

One of the tricks I have used to proceed in my journey is to visualize what I want my life to look like then work towards that vision. When I was working towards decluttering my room, I envisioned what I wanted it to look like. I wanted clear counters, nothing on the floor and the bookshelf to be organized. I visualized it. Then I got to work creating my vision and getting rid of anything that wasn't in the vision.

You can do this exercise for your home, for your health, for your finances and for your future goals. Make sure it's your vision of how you want things to be. Don't visualize someone else's life. Visualize yours.

Road Maps

This book is split into three sections. We have STOP, REDUCE and MAINTAIN. Each section is designed to help you get your life together. STOP gives you tips on stopping the chaos in its tracks. REDUCE gives you tips on decluttering different areas of your life. MAINTAIN gives you tips on maintaining your new lifestyle and how to keep improving.

In these sections are the main themes. If you don't want to overhaul your entire life at once, but prefer to tackle one area at a time, these roadmaps will show you what pages to follow to get the advice that you need.

Where Would You Like to Start?

SHOPPING	35, 71, 126 - 129
PHYSICAL CLUTTER	40, 41, 72 - 87, 130, 131-132
DIGITAL CLUTTER	42-46, 88-95, 131-134
HEALTH	47-49, 96-101, 135-138
FINANCES	50-53, 102-107, 139-141
RELATIONSHIPS	54, 108, 109, 142, 143
COMMITMENTS	55-60, 110, 111, 144-146
PERSONAL GROWTH	61, 112-114, 147

Companion Website

This book has a companion website that offers summaries, resources, checklists and other minimalist's advice on topics. I invite you to check out the website if my ideas throughout this book don't suit you. There might be another method or another voice that can help you achieve a goal.

Go to simplyminimal.life for more minimalism.

Marie

Entrepreneur and Leader of WomenMake.com

@marie_dm_ - Twitter

A few years ago, I wanted to change a few things in my life regarding my lifestyle. In order to be more healthy, I started with food. I decided to eat less processed products (microwaved meals, ready-cooked food, etc.), eat more vegetables and organic food. This also means I had to cook more.

Then I started to take an interest in ecology. I became vegetarian, slowly bought fewer things, especially packaged stuff (since it means more waste), started to make some of my cosmetics, got rid of all chemical stuff (especially household products). That's what slowly brought me to minimalism. So I'm not an extremist but for me, it meant to get rid of useless things (or at least not buying new ones when not necessary). Anyway, I always felt more relaxed when not having an apartment full of stuff.

Then a few months ago, I left my apartment and moved from Paris to become a nomad. I had to get rid of a lot of stuff. I can't carry many things with me so it was more of a step into minimalism.

Now I'm not saying I will never get an accommodation later but it will definitely be minimalist. Just a few things. I still have some furniture stored somewhere that I didn't sell. But I definitely feel freer. Actually, I think that's the most important: freedom. You're free cause you don't have expensive stuff to worry about.

You're free cause you don't need as much as before. You don't feel tied to material things. You're free cause you can leave quickly from place to place since you don't have to carry anything with you.

Stop

Stop The Madness

In this part of the book, we are going to stop the madness. It is important to stop the madness before going forward because if you don't learn to stop the madness, you will never fix the madness. All your efforts will be pointless because the madness will keep on piling up. The madness is everything that is making your life busy, chaotic and stressful.

In this part of the book, we are going to stop shopping. We are going to introduce a spending freeze so you can learn how to not spend impulsively. We are going to stop accepting every invite and actually consider what events we will like to attend. We're going to stop being on the internet every second of the day. These days we are glued to our phones and we're not seeing the beauty of life as it should be seen. We're going to stop hanging out with people we dislike and who bring us down with negativity. And we are going to stop unhealthy habits such as eating junk food and spending our whole paycheck.

The benefits of this part of the book should be more money in your pocket, more time in your schedule and less stress on your mind. Let's get started.

Stop Shopping

Shopping. Shopping is essentially how most of us got here in the first place. We live in a very consumerist world where everyone "has" to have the latest gadgets, the fastest cars, the biggest houses, the latest fashion and the highest corporate positions.

People love to go shopping as a hobby. Teenagers hang out at shopping malls. We love to walk aimlessly down aisles at stores. And, we can't make a trip without purchasing something.

The sad part is that most of our purchases end up staying in our lives. They take over the house, the car, the purse and attics, sheds, basements and garages. A lot of things sit around collecting dust because they haven't been used in years and probably won't ever be used again because the owner forgot about it, found something more useful or found out that they really didn't like it once they bought it.

And yet, we keep shopping. We keep bringing things home to sit around. It causes us clutter, and it makes our money go away. Those purchases could've been used for something more meaningful and useful.

How do we deal with our shopping tendencies? The first challenge of this book is to implement a spending freeze. This will teach you to think about items before wasting money. It will teach you that you don't need to buy something new if an issue pops up because you may have everything you need already on hand. This will teach you to be mindful of your things and to take care of your possessions. This alone will help put a stop to additional clutter.

So, what do we do? Pick a time frame that you are comfortable with. You may start off with a week to see how things go and then bump it up to a month. The end goal of the spending freeze is to stop spending money on things you don't absolutely and truly need or things that you will never use or enjoy. If after the week, you find yourself buying 3 pairs of shoes that were on sale when you already have 30 pairs at home, you did not complete the goal. So, do it again for longer.

Shopping is not only stealing our money, but sometimes impulsive shopping is a sign of an underlying issue. Just like when people turn to drugs or food when they can't cope with stress, people can also turn to shopping. If this is you, taking a spending freeze will greatly benefit you. You can learn your triggers and how to deal with them in healthy ways.

Spending freezes can overwhelm a lot of people.

Shopping has been ingrained in us since we were born. We are struck with advertisements every single day. If a spending freeze scares you, start out small. Do it for a week and then work your way up to a point to where by the end of the spending freeze, you don't feel the need to shop impulsively anymore.

The point of this isn't to stop buying things forever, but to see that you are buying unimportant, non-essential items that are not being used, taking up space and costing you money. A spending freeze is a great exercise to find out the items you truly need in your life.

what am i allowed to buy?

You have to buy things to survive. For example, food, toiletries and shelter all need to be bought in order to live and be hygienic.

During your spending freeze, you are allowed to buy essentials. You are also allowed to replace items that need to be replaced such as light bulbs.

Shopping is often used as a band-aid or a social activity. It can be a stress-reliever or it can give you some short-term pleasure with instant gratification. Instant gratification is when you want something and you have to have it as soon as possible. You want yours wants to be fulfilled without any delays. This often happens when shopping because we are exposed to so many cool and pretty things that we "gotta have!" And, since the item that we want is in reach and the money is in our hands, we usually fulfill ours wants a lot quicker. But, that pleasure high of having our wants met usually dies by the time we get home. Then we're wanting the next thing.

We can overcome instant gratification by delaying the time in which we get the things we want. Half the time, if you give yourself time to calm down over the coolness of an object, you'll find that you wouldn't really have much use for the object at all or you might find that you actually don't want it. So, wait as long as you can before buying things that you want.

If you are using shopping as a leisure activity or if you're faced with friends wanting to go on a shopping spree, consider doing one of these things instead:

- Suggest another activity. See if they'll go for a picnic or a Netflix and chill session.
- Leave your wallet at home. You can still enjoy the experience of hanging out with friends without having to break your freeze.
- Look for only things you need. Bring a list and

only enough money to purchase the items on the list.

Shopping isn't bad. We need to shop to survive and our economy needs shoppers to get it going. But, looking at our lives, it can be causing some issues that can be stopped if we take some time to look at the effects shopping causes us. Take note of how many little items that don't cost much add up in the long run. Also, take note of how those little items get little use and just sit in junk drawers until the end of time.

Are you wasting your money on items that serve no purpose for you? If you don't want to take a small spending freeze, I encourage to ask yourself questions the next time you are shopping. Ask yourself if you truly need that item, if it will serve a purpose in your life if you just want it to fill a void and how often are you going to use it? And, be honest with yourself.

Stop Collecting Things

Collections are an issue. They add to clutter. They take up space and they are usually not used. They usually just sit there and collect dust. Some collections are displayed, but most are stored. With bigger collections, you need to have more space dedicated to it. Space that now cannot be used for something useful.

If you are not actively using the collections, if they are not providing any value to you and if you don't absolutely love them enough that you will display them, you should think about getting rid of them. Collections are okay if they are giving you value. Just keep the number of different collections to a minimum and make sure every item is used or loved.

Stop Accepting Things

There will be many times where friends and family offer to give you items or even buy items for you. A lot of the times we accept these things because we are thankful that our loved one is being so nice and thoughtful towards us. We might feel guilty by saying no. And sometimes we feel pressured by that person to take it.

Before accepting these items, however, you need to think about this decision. Accepting something that you don't want or need will add to the clutter that you are trying to get rid of. Then when you decide to no longer keep it, you might feel more guilt because you are getting rid of a gift that so-and-so gave you.

It's always better to snip this in the bud and kindly decline their offer. You may even say, "thank you so much for thinking of me, but I really have no use for this. Is there someone else you can give it to?"

Stop Taking Excessive Photos

We are living in an era where is it is extremely easy to snap a photo and post it online. Just a short time ago, all we had to deal with were disposable cameras, scanners and a desktop computer in order to post an image online. Nowadays, we can as do everything from our smartphones. We're in a selfie nation where everyone takes selfies every day and post them on Instagram, Facebook, Twitter and Tumblr. But have you checked your phone's memory card lately? Are you constantly having to delete things in order to download an app because you're out of space? It may be because you are taking excessive amounts of photos. Now I'm not saying to stop taking selfies. Because who doesn't like selfies? I'm saying that when you go on vacation or out somewhere on a trip or see something so beautiful that you want to capture the moment, to capture the memory of it, don't take five or ten photos of it trying to get the perfect shot. When you only need one photo.

That sunset is going to look the same in every single photo of every single one of those ten pictures. One would do just fine. Plus it's take up a lot of time trying to get the perfect picture. And angle and exposure. When you could have been taken the time to actually admire that moment with your own eyes. One snap and that's enough to capture the moment. You don't need ten pictures.

Stop Being on the Internet Every Second of Every Day

Nowadays it's really hard to get our nose out of our phones. I get it. It's a wonderful miraculous thing that has come to our world. Everything is on the screen. Everything that we ever wondered is just a search away. It's literally all in the palm of our hands in our smartphones.

I get it. It's really incredible. And I am actually like many of you obsessed with it, but constantly having our phones in our noses can be impactful to our lives. We can miss out on moments. We can miss out on the beauty of nature. If you're walking somewhere you can now see everyone walking with their heads bent down to their phones. They don't even look at the sky anymore.

My Challenge For You

Take a day to go completely screen free. Do it on the weekend, so it doesn't interfere with work. And just use that day to relax. Read a book that isn't an ebook, go for a walk, play with your kids, play with your pets, or go outside and have a cook-off. A bake-a-thon does something that doesn't involve the Internet or a screen. And, crafts and puzzles are actually fun leisure activities.

Also, do the same with your TV. Ditch the TV for one day. And, if this is too hard, try going a week with limited screen time. Try leaving your phone at home when you go run errands all day. Just to see that you do not need to have it with you at all times.

Stop Bookmarking Everything

I don't know about you, but I have a habit of bookmarking everything. Every article I like, every article that I didn't read but wanted to, websites that were cool, websites that were pretty, the advice I will never follow, products that would be awesome to buy, blogs I wanted to keep up on, etc.

Not only was this too excessive, but I never went back in to look at the content. It just stayed in my bookmark folders for years. A lot of the stuff, I would just remember the URL and often I would just use google if I forgot. And when I did need something from the bookmarks it was a mess trying to find something in there due to all the clutter.

So, I bet you don't care for about 90% of your bookmarks. Think about that. Go through your bookmarks and declutter them. Clutter in bookmarks makes it harder to actually find the bookmarks that matter.

Stop Eating Junk Food and Commit to Healthier Snacks

Junk food isn't worth it. The processed garbage, the chemicals, the trans fat, oils and sugar are so not good for you. Most of us know this, yet we continue to digest these creations. Not only is it putting a damper on your health, but it's putting a damper on your finances and your energy.

When you are having sugar highs, spikes in insulin and crashes, you are not giving yourself the optimal energy it needs for the day. I'm not saying to ban your favorite snacks forever, but do limit and only consume occasionally. Weight gain and health issues put our mental health on the line and we can become at risk for depression which will not be helpful in making sure we are living happy positive lives.

Instead of daily junk food, try replacing it with fresh vegetables. Snack on vegetables and some healthy dips to get a good spike in energy and some extra minerals in your blood system.

Stop Drinking Soda

Soda is another health hazard that you should take steps to avoid. Soda is especially horrible towards your health because the sugar and caffeine create addictive side-effects. You begin to crave soda and want it all the time. Just like a drug addiction, quitting soda is a tough feat. It's going to take some willpower and some strength, but once you overcome it, you will be better and know that you are not damaging your health with fizzy drinks anymore.

slowly stop

Take your time in quitting if you think cold-turkey isn't for you. If you currently drink two cans a day, try doing one can for a week then half a can then no cans.

replace soda with water

As you're quitting soda, up your water intake. You can get rid of a bad habit while replacing it with a good habit. A little trick to feeling like you're drinking soda, but really drinking water is to start drinking sparkling or seltzer water. A little carbonation feels just like soda, but is really good for you!

To save money on carbonated water, it might be a good investment to get a SodaStream. It's really great for carbonating water and will save you money in the long run.

Stop Adding Debt

Before you get your finances in order, be sure to not accept any more debt. Accepting more debt will only prolong the process. You should be wanting to get out of debt not get deeper and deeper. Whenever you come across purchases that you cannot afford without financing, do not purchase. If you cannot afford to pay it outright then you should not buy it. You can always wait on the purchase until you've saved up money, but going into debt is not a good plan.

This means that you shouldn't use credit lines as if it's free money. You shouldn't put yourself into situations that make you want to spend (see page 36 to learn about starting a spending freeze).

This means that you should not take out any loans. Mortgages, car loans, personal loans and student loans should be avoided at all costs if possible.

If you want to get your finances in order and get out of debt, then you must stop adding to the pile.

Stop Subscriptions

Go through bank statements and find recurring subscriptions. Can you get rid of these? Can you afford these? Why do you need these in your life? Unsubscribe to ones that are not serving you.

We see subscriptions everywhere from magazines, email lists, these new monthly subscription boxes, etc. With so many subscriptions at low prices sometimes we don't see the compounded expense. $5 here and $10 there every month adds up fast!

A way to stop these subscriptions from cluttering up your life with things and hogging your money is to go through your bank statements and find the recurring bills. Ask yourself these questions:

1. Is this absolutely necessary?
2. Can I ACTUALLY afford this?
3. Why did I bring this into my life?

If you don't like the answers, maybe it's time to let them go.

Stop Unnecessary Bills

Some bills we need like gas/electric and water. But other bills are what we think we need but are actually 100% unnecessary. We can survive without cable, internet, phone bills and car bills. Now some of these might be super important to you than others. For instance, if someone lives in a more rural area, living without a car might actually lessen their quality of life as opposed to someone living in a city with everything in walking distance. Getting rid of these types of bills will differ from person to person, but I invite you to sit back and really think about these items.

Getting rid of cable might give you back hours of your time to do something more productive or to schedule "me" time for yourself. Since the average person watches 5 hours of TV a day and spends about $60 a month on cable, cutting the cord could be beneficial to your life. Think of what that time and the extra money could get you. You could spend the time and money on a hobby or on getting a monthly massage or facial.

Stop Spending More Than You Earn

Spending more than you earn is the number one reason why people struggle financially. Personal finance is super-easy math. There's money you make. There's money you spend. If you spend more than you make, you'll go into debt. If you make more than you spend, you'll have money left over. If you spend the same as what you make, you may be okay, but might have the feeling of living paycheck to paycheck and never really get ahead or have a savings for things.

I know some people just do not make enough to cover their expenses. I know poverty is a real thing. I grew up in poverty. I know some people have made past mistakes that have taken them into debt and are struggling to get out of it.

I understand and I know personal finance is super-easy math, but life is super complicated.

You need to have a close look into your finances and see where you can cut back and then cut back. If need be, you may have to bring in more income. Reread pages 36 and 51 - 52 to see where you can save money, and read pages 140 - 141 to see how to bring more in.

Stop Hanging Around Toxic People

We all have one person that we can't stand to be around. But you just really can't get rid of them because they're constantly there. Sometimes you just have to cut toxic people off. So you can be happy. Sometimes it's a person that walks all over you. Expects you to do everything for them with nothing in return. This is easier said than done.

Breaking off from people can be hard, so here are a couple ideas:

- Slowly say no when they ask you to hang out or come over.

- If you guys usually hang out three times a week, bring it down to two times a week and then into one and then only once in a while.

- Just say, "Hey, here are some things that are bothering me about you. And, I'm not trying to be mean, but I can't work on myself if you're doing this and that. You are bringing me down."

There's no perfect answer for your situation. But, if you have a person bringing you down, stop hanging around them.

Stop Accepting Every Invite

These days our calendars are filled to the point where there's no time left to spare for ourselves. Every day it's a party here. A gathering there. And we accept all of them. We say yes to all. And we mark it down on our calendars. However, we accept too much. Our calendars are overfilled with invites and commitments and responsibilities. Not only are we accepting the social gatherings on top of our work commitments and family obligations, we are accepting these invites over our personal time.

And some of the time, these invites do not make us happy at all. We may accept them just to be nice, out of courtesy. We say yes to a social gathering where we know that we're going to be bored or probably the third wheel. And honestly, you would rather just be at home in bed reading a good book. So we are going to go through a process where we stop accepting every invite and start scheduling some personal time.

The Declining Challenge

Try this for a week: Whenever someone invites

you somewhere, sit back. Do not give them an answer right away. Give yourself some time to think about it and only if you would truly be happy by going to this place, accept it. Otherwise, it's OK to say, "no." Or, try suggesting something else instead. Once you get in the habit of doing this. you start to see some extra time and you will start doing more activities that you enjoy.

Stop Accepting New Responsibilities

Sometimes you can be stressed out because you have too many responsibilities. A lot of times people accept and gain responsibilities because either they have to, want to or want to be nice and help another person.

If there are responsibilities that are causing you stress, stop them if possible. You don't have to do everything or help everyone especially if it's taking a toll on you.

Stop Doing Things
That Are Not Bringing You Joy

I bet every day you find yourself groaning and complaining about something. Maybe it's about a job, a chore, waking up early or doing an errand. There are some things that we must do. We have to wash our dishes and we have to work to live, but other things we can lessen or we can delegate to someone else or actually pay other people to do it. Laundry for example. You can pay someone else to do your laundry. Although there is a price tag, it could free up your time. So, it might be worth the price tag. Or, if you have older children, you could assign the chores you dislike to them!

Another thing is waking up early. A lot of people are not morning people. To get around this, you could work a job that offers a later shift. Maybe you're waking up earlier because you have a huge morning routine. You can pare down the routine by doing things the night before. If your morning routine currently involves getting an hour of exercise in, taking a shower, packing your lunch, getting your kids ready, walking the dog and leaving for the day. You can pare down your morning by exercising, showering and packing your lunch the night before. This way everything still gets done, but you can sleep in later in the mornings.

Here are some other things that we do that we may not like

doing things for others

It's really nice to do things for others. But, sometimes it gets to a point where it's too much especially when your one act of kindness turns into an expected chore.

doing things BECAUSE of others

A lot of people do things because it's what they think they should do. Society tells us what is normal and we need to do certain things so we can fit in.

One example is women shaving their legs. It's a normal thing to do. Almost all of us girls do it. But, ask yourself if you're doing it for yourself or for other people. Do you like shaving your legs? Same thing with makeup. If you don't enjoy putting makeup on or shaving don't. Don't do it for other people. Only do it for yourself.

If you don't enjoy doing things, don't do it. It's really that simple.

Working

We need to work to live and pay bills. But, we don't need to overwork ourselves especially if working is something that stresses us or it's something we generally don't like. But, how can you cut down on working? Cut down unnecessary bills and expenses. By cutting down on expenses, you can reduce the amount of money you need to live. Then, you can work less and still pay your bills. You can even make money from hobbies or get a different job that suits you.

Doing things you dislike puts stress on you. It will be better to not do them. So, whenever you are groaning and complaining about something, try to think about ways to make it easier or eliminate it completely. You can get your spouse and children to help you out with chores or hire a cleaning service once a week. Look into getting a dishwasher to cut down on dish cleaning. Stop doing things society tells you to do if you don't like it. There's always something you can do to make yourself a little bit happier.

Start Scheduling in Free Time

We all need time for ourselves. if we're too busy doing everything for others and neglect ourselves we will run into problems such as being burned out, stressed, fatigued and depressed.

Scheduling in some free time throughout the week is doable and not challenging. If you are struggling, try scheduling it on your appointment calendar and treat it as a priority appointment. You can even schedule in something like a 15-minute meditation session or a 20-minute hot shower. It doesn't have to be a large time commitment starting out.

Soon, as you are gaining time and accepting fewer responsibilities you can be able to squeeze in more you time to work on yourself, experience personal growth or just relax.

Becca Ehrlich
The Christian Minimalist
www.christainminimalism.com

My journey to minimalism was a gradual one. I remember over 10 years ago attending a weekend retreat, and looking in my suitcase. "This is so much simpler, just having the right amount of clothes and what I need for the weekend," I thought. "I wish I could live like this all the time." In the years following that retreat I found myself trying to get rid of some things over and over, but never really kicking my attachment to stuff and my habit of online shopping when I was bored or not feeling well.

Over the last decade, I've gone through some really rough stuff—my infant son died in 2014, and shortly after that I became very ill. My husband Will and I went to could figure out what was wrong with me. After years of medical testing, a surgery, and bouncing from doctor to doctor, we are finally figuring out how to manage my chronic illness. Due to the loss of our son, my health, and starting a new job after leaving a work situation that was making me unhappy and stressed, we have moved multiple times in the last 5 years, accumulating stuff along the way.

We moved in August of 2017 from a 3,000-square foot home in western New York that we owned (and eventually sold), to a small three-bedroom apartment in Pennsylvania. Most of our stuff ended up in a storage unit outside of town, and we shoved the rest of our stuff in every nook and cranny of the apartment. I felt like we were drowning in stuff. I was also figuring out that stress and emotional upset was a big trigger for my chronic illness, and I was struggling to find the best way to manage the stress in my life of changing jobs, moving, and managing my chronic illness.

A few months after the move, while browsing Netflix, I found and watched The Minimalists' (Joshua Fields Millburn and Ryan Nicodemus') documentary, Minimalism: A Documentary, and I knew right away that the Holy Spirit was speaking to me and that minimalism would be beneficial for both myself and my husband. I showed the documentary to Will, and he agreed and was immediately on board.

On the second viewing with Will, it struck me that both Joshua and Ryan talked about how people come to minimalism because they are looking for meaning in their lives. I remember turning to Will and saying: "Well, Christians know what that meaning is, it's Jesus! I wonder if anyone is writing about minimalism from a Christian perspective that we can read?"

Turns out, no one really is. The closest I could find was Joshua Becker, an amazing writer and blogger (and fellow pastor, actually!) who uses Biblical passages in his books, but most of his writing about minimalism is secular. I was craving more in-depth information about minimalism through a Christian lens, and it really didn't exist.

Thus, the existence of my blog. I knew I couldn't be the only one who wanted to talk about the intersection of minimalism and the Christian faith—and I wanted to share our Christian minimalism journey so that it could help others on their own journey. So, here we are!

Will and I started our minimalism journey at the beginning of 2018, and we are definitely a work in process. We are figuring out this minimalism thing as we go, and when I told Will about my blog idea, right away he offered to help me. So although I write all the content, he is the technological mastermind behind the running of the blog itself.

I am an ordained pastor in the Evangelical Lutheran Church in America (ELCA), one of the Lutheran denominations in the United States. I currently work as Associate Director of Admissions at United Lutheran Seminary (ULS), one of the seven seminaries of the ELCA. I am also working towards my doctoral degree in Christian Spirituality.

Before moving to Pennsylvania and working at ULS, I served as a parish pastor at two Lutheran churches in western New York State. I have two theological Masters degrees—a Master of Divinity (MDiv) from The Lutheran Theological Seminary at Philadelphia (one of the predecessor seminaries of ULS), and a Master of

Arts (MA) in Theology and Ministry from LaSalle University in Philadelphia. I also double-majored in Dance and Dramatic Arts Criticism (self-designed) in my Bachelor of Arts (BA) degree at Muhlenberg College in Allentown, PA, so performing arts, movies, theatre, and musical theatre are my jam.

I grew up in Albany, NY in an interfaith household (my mom is Roman Catholic and my dad is Jewish), and I currently live in Gettysburg, PA with my husband Will. Will works in technology ministry for the YouVersion Bible App, helping to reach people with the Word of God all over the world in over a thousand languages. He is also studying at ULS to become a Deacon in the ELCA. Will and I have been married since 2012, and I'm grateful to God every day for bringing us together.

Reduce

Get Things in Order

In the first section of this book, you have learned how to stop the madness. You have learned how to stop shopping impulsively, how to stop accepting every invite that comes your way, how to stop the excessive photos and internet clutter.

Now, you're spending less time on the internet and more time with the people you love. You are not doing things that do not bring a smile to your face. And maybe, you have found some time for yourself.

The next section of this book is going to teach you how to get things in order. You're going to rid your life of material possessions that don't give you value or joy. From your clothes to your paper clutter to your kitchen and bathroom, this next section is going to give you the motivation and the push to tackle your clutter. The section will also touch on simplifying your diet, evaluating relationships and learning how to keep stress at bay.

So, let's get things in order.

Start Thinking About Purchases

We are now in the age where everything we ever wanted is one click away. We have the world at our fingertips and all we need to do is hand over our money. Most of these things have gotten you to this point in the first place. A lot of these just add to your clutter and are not used or serving you.

Before spending money on purchases give yourself time to think about them and ask yourself if you truly will use it and love it. A helpful hint is to delete your payment information on websites like Amazon. That way you will have to log in all your information again to make a purchase. The harder it is to buy, the less likely you'll want to go through the whole process.

This is how online stores are so convenient because making buying easy is a good business model. People love not working for what they want.

Your Things

You want to get order in your life. You're sick of the clutter, sick of cleaning the clutter, sick of seeing the clutter and you want it gone. You've been researching minimalism and have seen so many happy faces on people with less stuff. Well, it's your turn now. If you've completed the first section, you are a third of a way done. You're stopping the madness from coming in, and now it's time to purge what was already let in.

Ways to Dispose of Your Items

If you have finally gotten to a point where you have collected things you do not want anymore, it is time to dispose of your unwanted items.

I want to give you a short list of ways you can get rid of your stuff in an ethical manner.

Ethical Discarding Order

1. sell your items
2. give to a family who needs the items
3. donate items to charities or thrift stores
4. recycle items that are deemed recyclable
5. discard items in the trash. *Please do this only if the items are beyond repairable, usable or recyclable.

Disposing items in an ethical manner will keep your conscience in check and do good to others receiving your items.

Clothes

Everyone in the minimalist community loves to show off their wardrobes. Some participate in Project 333 where each season, you pick out 33 items from your wardrobe and only wear those items for 3 months. Some people have only 33 items in total. Some less and some more.

The goal isn't about numbers; it's about what you need. What clothes do you need to live your life? A stay-at-home mother is going to have a different wardrobe than a man who works as a farmer. Every circumstance is different, so we can't base our wardrobes off of someone else. A quick Google search will show you many wardrobes you can get inspiration from including capsule wardrobes.

A Capsule wardrobe is a small collection of clothes (usually around 10-50 items) that someone owns. This includes shoes and accessories and it's the only clothing the person owns. These collections are streamlined with pieces that are functional, versatile and can be worn in almost all situations and seasons of the year.

If this is something that sounds interesting to you, I encourage you to check them out, but you don't have to have a capsule wardrobe to be a minimalist. Purging your clothes is going to take a couple steps, and it's going to take a while. You have to locate all your clothes, try them on and decide whether they should stay in your life. Make sure you've set aside a couple hours to do this.

The Clothing Purge

step one: the cleaning

It'll be easier to go through your clothes on laundry day or the day after, so all your clothes are clean. But, you can just work with the dirty clothes by keeping them separate from the clean ones.

step two: the gathering

Take all your clothes, shoes and accessories and put them all together in the same area. Every single piece of clothing that belongs to you should be in this area. Don't forget about underwear, socks, gym clothes and specialized clothing such as bathrobes, belts, skates, soccer cleats and other accessories.

Make sure to set some time to find all your clothes. If later you find an article that was hidden in the attic or in some corner, you should think hard about donating it since it was clearly not on your mind.

step three: the sorting

Sort all the clothing into categories by type. Put

shirts with the shirts, put shorts with the shorts and put socks with the socks. This will give you a visual on how much of each item you actually have. It may also be helpful if you separate the pile further such as pajama shirts in one pile, workout shirts in another and regular shirts in a third.

step four: passing the test

The internet is scoured with different testing variables. In the Marie Kondo Method, you must hold each item as ask yourself if the piece brings you joy. Yes? Keep it. No? Toss it. Others want you to try on every single piece and see what looks and feels good on you.

I think these are all great ideas, but very time-consuming. If you want to take the above suggestions, go for it! But, here were my testing points when I was purging my clothes:

Have I worn this in the past 3 months? If not, why? If the answers were: I forgot about it, I don't really reach for it or I'm waiting for the right moment, I tossed it.

Here are some other questions I asked myself:

- If this were my only piece of clothing, would I want to wear it all the time?
- Is it comfy, versatile and can I wear it with almost

everything?

Make your own test and don't give any piece of clothing any mercy. If it fails a test, toss it. If you can't find three outfits for it go with, get rid of it. How you go about is up to you and how you feel you should handle the situation.

step five: the purge

As you are taking each piece of clothing through your test, start to make piles. If a shirt fails the test, see if you are able to donate it and put in it a donation pile. If you are able to sell it, put it in a sell pile. Then, when you're done going through all your clothes, take the failed items and put them up for sale or donation. If there are clothes that are too worn down, see if you can make something out it before throwing it away. Cotton socks can be made into nice rags for cleaning as an example.

step six: repeat

Repeat these steps every so often. You'll be surprised that you still keep finding things you are no longer using after the first round. You may have even found a pile of clothes in a hidden location somewhere. Pick a time frame (every month, every season, every 6 months) and go at it again until you are happy with your wardrobe.

Afterward

After purging your wardrobe you may find that now you are lacking in clothing areas. You might have gotten rid of all your jeans because they were too big, or all your socks may have had holes in them. In this case, write down the articles that you truly need and don't have. Next time if friends invite you shopping, you can have something to look and shop for. If you are doing a spending freeze add these items to your exceptions list. Make sure that the next pieces of clothing you bring in your life will serve you well. Look for clothes of high quality, in a style that you like and that makes you feel good when you wear them. This will mean spending a little more money from time to time. But, investing in a piece of clothing that will last you a very long time saves money in the long run.

There are many stores out that make a profit on "fast fashion." These clothes are cheaply made and are meant to have a short lifespan, so customers will come back again and again to buy the next thing. The price tag may be cheap up front, but over time the cost of buying these items add up.

Papers

Papers are one of these things that quickly multiply in a short amount of time. We get mail every day, we get papers from doctors appointments, schools and receipts when shopping. We already talked about stopping the madness. If you have eliminated as much paper coming in as you can then it's time to declutter what you already have. Start by gathering every piece of paper you can find.

Our goal is to rid ourselves with as much paper clutter as possible. Figure out what's truly important then shred and recycle the rest. Get rid of any "reference" paper with information that is easily found on the internet. Get rid of any paper that you haven't looked at in a year. You can scan the important papers and shred and recycle those too. But, make sure to keep tax documents for up to seven years. We don't want to make the IRS unhappy now.

After eliminating paper clutter, you'll feel so much freer. Paperweights are so heavy! If you're lucky you may be able to declutter more than just paper; maybe you're able to get rid of a file cabinet as well!

Kitchen Items

Kitchen gadgets are a problem. There are whole stores dedicated to these little items that claim to make cooking easier. Sometimes, they make things more complicated!

If you own any kitchen gadgets, really ask yourself if you're using them. Then ask yourself if it's really saving you time by using it.

Other areas of the kitchen that should be addressed are the pots and pans phenomenon. Why do we have several sets of pots and pans? You can't possibly use them all at once with just one stove. And how many baking sheets do you need? Or casserole dishes?

Look around your kitchen and take inventory. What do you never use? Are there things hiding deep within the bottom cupboard that you didn't remember you had? Get rid of everything you are not using.

And what about dishes? Plates, bowls, cups, spoons, forks and knives. Oh, my! There's a lot of cupboard space being dominated by dishes. Use the same methods you've been using to declutter. Go through everything and get rid of everything you're not using. Get rid of multiple sets. Only keep 2 dish items per family member and a few for guests. It's up to you, but only keep what you truly need.

Look into getting rid of those old appliances that are in the back of the cabinet and are never used. Think about getting rid of dishes that are holiday themed and are only used once a year. Get rid of anything you haven't used in a year. Duplicates need to go!

If you want fewer dishes to wash, you should own fewer dishes. Sounds weird, but it's true! The more dishes you keep the more tempting it is to reach for a clean dish while there's a sink full of dirty dishes. Pretty soon every dish is dirty and doing dishes is a full-day job! Fewer dishes = fewer dishes to do.

Just think about roomy cabinets and cleared counters and then declutter!

Bathroom and Linen

Bathroom items, particularly linen can multiply before you know it. It doesn't help that there are entire storage areas dedicated to these things like under the bathroom sink and linen closets.

I have witnessed this several times over my life when I go looking for a band-aid or new bottle of shampoo and stumble upon an entire civilization of products. Bottles everywhere, half-used lotions and gels, medicines, boxes of toothpaste, hair products, teeth products, face products, etc.

It's an evasion of products and it's so unorganized. It's just clutter. And most of the stuff is not being used. Then, there's the linen.

We have stacks of towels, rags, sheets, pillowcases and even curtains! All crammed into these spaces. How many towels does a person need? How many sheets does a bed need?

To get these places under control, you need to declutter and minimize. Just the same as any area of this book: Go through everything, ask yourself if you use it or need it, then get rid of everything you are not using.

To give you some ideas on where to start:

- Only keep two sets of towels per family member
- Limit bathroom decorations
- Get rid of expired products
- Get rid of products that suck. Don't feel guilty about unused products. Get rid of them.
- Get rid of linens that have been stored longer than a year
- Only keep two sets of linen per bed

Make sure to tackle your linen closet (if you have one), under the sink, the medicine cabinet and any other storage in the bathroom such as a small cabinet or storage over the toilet.

Think about how organized and spacious your bathroom can be! After getting rid of everything you are not needing, you won't have to knock over cans to get to the thing in the back of the closet again.

Random Possessions

Random possessions are things that cannot easily fit into a category like bathroom items or kitchen items. You might run across quite a few things that don't have a definitive place to go. One thing that comes to mind is furniture. You have furniture throughout your entire home not just in certain areas.

When you come across random items, decide whether or not to ditch it. Ask yourself if it's something you truly need, use or love. It may help to keep a donation/give-away box in each room while you are going through this process. It will be easy as you are going through things to be able to toss everything in one spot.

Once the box is full, it's easy to haul to a donation center or to sort through it to give things away or sell. This tip really helped me to not only get the unused stuff together but to get the items out of my life quickly. There's nothing more pressing than having a huge box of junk blocking your way to a door!

Sentimental Items

Sentimental items are the hardest category to tackle because these items have emotional attachments. These items, have deep meaning mainly pertaining to family, memories and huge life milestones.

It will not be easy dealing with sentimental items and you may want to keep all of them. But just like everything else, you shouldn't let these items have a hold on you or your life. You should go through the same process as everything else and see if you can get rid of any of these items.

Here are some tips for dealing with sentimental items and some tips on letting some of these items go:

- Save these items for last since this will be hard.
- Give yourself some time and slowly go through them. Let yourself process the memories.
- Keep only the items that are most important to YOU (not anyone else).
- Digitize as much as possible. Scan letters and cards. Take pictures of objects.

Sometimes other family members will give you sentimental items that were sentimental to them. You need to decide if you are actually the one finding value in the item and you're not just feeling guilty because of someone you know loved the item. It's okay to let the item go if you feel no emotions towards it. You may even be able to give it back or to someone else in the family who has emotional attachments to it.

Digitizing objects can let you keep them while also saving a ton of space. It can also give you a piece of mind that you can always see that knickknack again just in digital form.

Keep precious things that truly give you joy. Use these items as decoration. And if you're keeping the items just to store them out of sight, please reconsider giving them away. If you truly loved them, they would not be stuffed in a box somewhere for you to forget.

Decluttering Digital Items

It's so easy to build up the digital clutter because we physically cannot touch it and all the files and emails are so small that we can have millions of them on tiny devices. Digitizing items is a way to save physical safe and a way to be more eco-friendly, but sometimes it can go too far and become overwhelming and overbearing.

If you find yourself having a hard time locating files, having your computer or phone run out of space often, having your computer or phone run slower than usual or having your free storage in email or the cloud all used up, it may be time to declutter your digital space.

Here are some digital areas to think about:

- Computer files/folders
- Hard drives/thumb drives/flash drives
- Emails
- Photos
- Documents
- Bookmarks

Limit Distractions

Distractions are bad because we use them to procrastinate, to pacify ourselves. Distractions can take us away from important tasks and make us lose our focus.

Distractions are a waste of time. Not only do they make you waste hours doing them, but they can make the task at hand take twice as long. For example, if you're trying to work and you keep getting distracted by scrolling through Facebook, something that should have taken an hour now takes all day. You're choosing to procrastinate by focusing on a distraction.

We can use distractions as pacifiers or fill a void within ourselves. One example is the Netflix Binge. People are very open to admitting that they love to binge-watch shows on Netflix. I have done it myself. But, this is one big distraction that is taking away hours and hours from our lives. I started watching Netflix when I felt stressed about money. Watching the shows was a pacifier to me. So, I could ignore my problems for a few hours or days.

But, that's not a good thing to do. We can't run away from our problems or our to-do lists. I'm going to give you some tips on how to limit distractions.

delete social media apps from your phone

There's an app for everything. Apps are awesome. They are entertaining. They are useful. But, many of them are big distractions. Especially social media apps. How much time do you spend scrolling through feeds? Everyone has their vice rather it's Facebook, Instagram or Twitter. These social media apps have enough content that you can spend your whole day scrolling on them.

If you are getting distracted by these apps or you find yourself spending way too much time on them, I encourage you to delete them off your phone. You can still access them through the internet browser on your phone, but the extra steps to get to the website, will cause a big inconvenience and you will slowly stop checking them all the time.

I recommend deleting all the social media from your phone and scheduling a time to go enjoy them like at night before bed. This will also open up storage space on your phone for apps that are really useful for you. Extra space will also make your phone run faster. There are so many pluses to this!

find a quiet space

Finding a quiet space will limit distractions of other people and noise. Having a little space to yourself for awhile will boost your productivity for the tasks at hand.

Here are some ideas on where to find a quiet space and how you can make one:

- An extra bedroom in your house.
- A quiet corner in your room. Set up a cozy little desk and you're all set!
- The library. The library is the perfect quiet place if you need a few hours to work or to have time for yourself.
- Venture outside. There may be a porch, balcony or a picnic area next to a beautiful pond that is calling your name.
- Your local coffee shop. These tend to be a little loud, but if you're okay with a little coffee shop ambiance, it may be a good fit for you!

create a routine

Make a schedule or routine that allows for things you want to work on. If you love your hobby – for example, knitting – but you feel like you never have time for it, creating a daily routine that gives you a block of time to focus on your hobby is a good idea. This way, you're not always trying to squeeze it in, and realizing that you just don't have the time.

Creating a routine and following it will give you more time. You will know exactly what you're doing throughout the day and you are not scrambling around figuring out what you should be doing. Creating a routine will prevent distractions from popping up. If you're supposed to exercise at 5 pm every day, you won't have time to sit and watch TV because you already committed yourself to workout.

turn off notifications

If you have decided to keep the apps on your phone, the easiest thing to do to keep apps from distracting you would be to turn the notifications off. You can automatically turn off app notifications from your settings section on your phone. But, for some phones, you may have to manually turn notifications off for each app.

In your settings on your phone, look for the "Applications" section (or just "Apps") and click on each app to turn off notifications. While you're at it, try to turn notification SOUNDS off as well. Not only are notifications a visual distraction, they are an auditory distraction.

How are you supposed to do things you're supposed to be doing when you're constantly hearing the dings? Get rid of notifications!

shut down email

Email is one of the biggest distractions because there are constantly coming into your inbox throughout the day. A lot of people are stressed over email because they don't want to miss anything important so they check their emails all the time.

To limit this big distraction, I would look at email as an appointment and schedule it in in your day. Every day at 2 o'clock you have a meeting with email.

remove clutter

Clutter is a big distraction. How can you focus on your work when your desk is a mess? When you are dealing with work that is challenging, your mind is going to want to find a way out of it and your mind will make chores and cleaning seem like so much fun.

If you clear your clutter and get rid of it for good by getting rid of belongings that don't make you happy or serve a purpose you will limit this distraction. This will take some time beforehand, but as you pare down your possessions and simplify your life, lots of clutter will become just a memory.

Unsubscribing and Unfollowing

Social media is a lot to handle. There's information overload. There's constant news; constant refreshes. It's just too time-consuming. It's distractions and time wasters. Most cluttered feeds are made up of accounts and information that are not important to you.

I have a social media challenge for you. Go to every social media channel you visit often and unfollow, unsubscribe and unlike all accounts, people, pages and channels that you are currently getting updates from.

Once you're done with the unfollowing, look at your feeds and notice how empty and calm they are. I recommend waiting at least 2 days before subscribing again to give your brain a detox. After your detox period, slowly subscribe to the channels and accounts that you've genuinely missed the content of.

Most likely all the cluttered accounts will go unremembered and your feeds will be full of useful and loved content that you can truly enjoy. Another tip in this area if you don't want to unfriend everyone (especially friends and family) is to unfollow or mute them. Facebook allows you to unfollow updates of people without unfriending them and Twitter allows you to mute accounts without unfollowing them.

Cleaning up your feed will make you less stressed, less worried about missing an update, give you fewer notifications and save you time scrolling. If you take it a step further, only follow people that inspire you to better your life. You can jump to page 134 to learn more about that!

Simplify Your Health

Another area of our lives that we should focus on is our health. We are bombarded with information every single day to help improve our health, but the information can be overwhelming, confusing, contradicting and not true. There are businesses trying to make profits off of your health. There is a huge weight-loss industry with over a thousand different vitamins, pills, shakes, drinks, meal replacements, bars, powders, programs and books claiming they have the magic answer to weight-loss and health.

In this section, I am going to go over the importance of diet and exercise and how you can simplify what you're doing now so that your health can be your number one priority, but not that much of a hassle.

diet

When I say diet, I don't mean restricting or counting calories. I mean our eating habits and what type of food we should consume to survive, be healthy and be full.

The Standard American Diet (SAD) is a sad diet. People are lacing their foods with a lot of grease, oil, sugar and animal fat. It's unhealthy. Simplifying our diets will make us feel better as we gain control over other parts of our lives.

The ultimate minimalist diet is raw veganism. Although it is not the most sustainable for the average person, it's super simple. All you eat is fruit, vegetables, nuts and seeds. That's all you have to focus on. Very simple. Very minimal. You don't even have to cook!

I'm not going to persuade you to give up warm food for cold, crunchy goodness. But, I am going to use some of the principles of the raw vegan diet to help you simplify your own diet:

Limit Animal Products

I don't know why we are still eating innocent animals. We do not need them for protein. Vegetables contain enough protein for us. We do not need them for iron. Legumes contain enough iron for us. We may need them for B12, but animals get their B12 from eating plants.

It's your choice whether to eat animals or not, but eating animals increases your risk for many diseases including heart disease, cancers, diabetes, high blood pressure, etc. Reading How Not to Die by Dr. Michael Greger shows research study after research study of evidence that consuming animals is not good for us. If you don't want to purchase the book, try finding it at the library or watching videos on Nutrition-Facts.org to see for yourself.

I will warn you though, the book is a thick monster that dives into topics of biology, anatomy and dietary nutrition.

Limiting animal products including meat, dairy (milk, cheese, yogurt, etc), eggs, whey, oil and honey will put your health in a step in the right direction. It will also save you a lot of money. Many claim eating healthy is so expensive, but a diet full of meat is actually the most costly. According to CentSai.com, a meat eater spends about $8 more on food a day. That adds up to $2,920 extra dollars a year spent on meat.

Limit Processed Foods

Most processed foods have a boatload of chemicals and most have addictive properties. It's best to steer clear of these foods as much as possible.

You can try swapping processed food with better options. Processed snack foods can be swapped for fruits and vegetables or a fun plant-based, homemade recipe! Google has a million healthy treat recipes for you to try. Just search, "plant-based snacks." Processed meals like microwave dinners can be swapped for beans, grains, vegetables, potatoes, soups, salads, veggie burgers, veggie chili, veggie spaghetti, vegetable pizza, burritos, etc. There are endless possibilities for dinner that are yummy, healthy and fresh!

Make More Food At Home

If we are trying to save time, then why should you cook at home? Well, this is up to you. There's a catch 22 here. You can save time by buying convenient meals, but it'll cost more money. Or, you can save money by cooking at home, but it'll waste some of your time.

Although cooking fresh, healthy meals for yourself will never be a waste of time. This way you can control the ingredients and the freshness of the ingredients.

To save some time by cooking at home, try meal prepping and cooking a bunch of meals for the week or to freeze for later. Invest in a rice cooker or Instant Pot to pressure cook food in a snap. Or get a crock-pot and prep dinner in the morning and have a hot meal at dinner time.

Focus on Plants

As you do your shopping, as you prepare your meals and as you are putting food into your body, focus on plants. Ask yourself if you're eating plant food or if you're eating processed goo. The more plant food you put in your body, the better your health will be.

exercise

Exercise depends on you. If you love to exercise and want to do it for hours every day, go for it! You're great. But this section is for people who don't particularly love exercising but know they need to do it to stay healthy and want to do it in a very minimalist way.

Minimalist Workouts

Minimalist workouts include exercises that are free (or with little investment), that you can do practically anywhere and are fun!

- Walking. Walking can be enjoyed with a friend, with a pup or with an awesome podcast.
- Jump roping. Bring back the childhood days, or warm-up like a boxer by buying a jump-rope.
- Yoga. There are so many free yoga workout videos on YouTube. You just need a soft place for posing.
- Interval Training. This can be in any activity really, but my favorite is running with the Zombies Run! App.
- Dancing. Plenty of dancing workout videos are on

YouTube or you can do it old-fashioned by play-ing music and diving right in.

- Strength training with body weight. Not particu-larly fun, but creating a workout, strength train-ing routine without equipment, can get you into shape quicker with shorter workouts.
- Hiking. Picking a beautiful park and just go en-joy.
- Biking. Investing in a bike can be fun! You can get around faster than walking and you might be able to commute to work or the grocery store and save on gas!

Those are some of my exercise ideas that are minimal. It is recommended that you get 90 minutes of moderate-intensity exercise or 40 minutes of vigor-ous-intensity exercise a day.

Also, disclaimer, I'm not a doctor or a nutrition-ist, so be sure to see to see a doctor before starting a new eating or exercise plan. Especially if you are facing an illness or taking medication!

Get Out of Debt

Getting out of debt as quickly as possible not only takes a huge burden off your shoulders, but it actually saves you a lot of money. The more you have debt, the more interest adds up and the more money you have to pay. Interest is an evil all on its own. Not only do you have to pay back the principal amount you borrowed but you also have to pay more money on top of it. And your debt keeps growing every single day.

To save money in the long run and to stop paying more and more money, try to get out of debt as soon as possible. There are a lot of articles out there on the best way to get out of debt. And they all are awesome because getting out of debt is simple. You simply pay it off. So, all the methods out there work, but since there's so many, it's overwhelming. So I am going to give you three steps to paying off debt fast.

step 1: any extra leftover money every month put towards debt.

This doesn't mean to spend spend spend throughout the month and give whatever is left towards debt. It means to follow your money plan and anything left over gets put towards debt. If you are doing a spending freeze from page 36 then you are well on your way to having some extra money every month.

step 2: pay off monthly debt first.

If you have debt bills that occur every month like car payments, credit cards balances and student loans, pay these down first before any other debt. Once you pay off monthly debt, you will free up, even more, money every month to put towards more debt.

step 3: pay off everything else.

After freeing up money by paying down your monthly debts, you can now pay off any other debts such as things in collections, family debts and medical bills.

Saving and cutting expenses is one side of the story of finding extra money. The other way is making more money. Selling items, doing side-gigs, starting a business, getting a temporary, second job or adding multiple streams of income (discussed on page 140) are just some ways to make the extra money you need to pay down your debts.

Set Up Retirement

Retirement is an important investment you should be doing. This buildup of cash will help you live comfortably in the later years of life when you no longer want to work. It should be a priority and a must.

The easiest way to set up a retirement account is with your employer. A lot of companies even match your money! That is free money! You should take complete advantage of this.

If you are self-employed or if your employer doesn't offer a 401k plan, then your next bet is setting up a Roth IRA with a brokerage. Roth IRA stands for Roth Independent Retirement Account. This is an account that acts similar to a 401k plan. You are able to save for retirement and you can only access the money when you retire.

how much money should i contribute

This depends on your goals. Do you want to retire a millionaire? Do you just want to be comfortable? Or do you want to spend most of your money now and just have enough later on?

If you want to be rich, save 20% of your income

into your retirement account. If you want the bare minimum, don't go lower than 5%.

brokerage

My favorite brokerage is the app Betterment. It's super quick and easy to set up Roth IRAs and they are very helpful in choosing the best one for you. The Acorns app, originally an investing app, is also coming out with a program called Acorns Later. I recommend either of these companies if you cannot get a 401k plan.

some helpful books on this topic are:

- I Will Teach You to be Rich – Ramit Sethi
- Automatic Millionaire – David Bach

These books are loaded with other helpful personal finance advice too. The number one lesson I've learned is although it's never too late to start saving for retirement, the younger you start, the more financial gain you will receive.

So start saving for retirement NOW.

Set Up an Emergency Fund

All the money experts shove this piece of advice down your throat and it's such a good piece of advice, but are you actually following it? Do you have some money set aside for emergencies? Yes? Good. You're on track. Read below to see how far on track you are. If your answer is "no", keep reading.

An emergency fund can save your life. Last year, my new-to-me car of just one year broke down for the millionth time. This time, for the junkyard. I was sold a lemon and it was breaking down every other month. So, this time, we had to buy a new car or my husband wouldn't be able to go to work and we'd be stranding without half our income.

So, my whole paycheck had to go towards a down payment. We didn't have any other choice and we suffered because of it. If we had an emergency fund, however, this whole ordeal would have been less of a burden. Okay, great right? Just get an emergency fund. Where am I going to get the money? Well, hopefully by following the principles of this book, you are starting to save some money from your life's adventures. And if not, it's not hard to start slowly building an emergency fund.

Start slowly with an amount such as $20 a month. Something doable. Then automate it. If you have your banking set up for automatic withdraws into a savings account every month or every paycheck, it will take the burden off of you to remember to transfer the funds.

It may even stop you from spending it on something else!

After a few months of saving the initial savings goal every month, try to up the amount. You may find that you can save more than you thought you could. Use raises, tax refunds or other events that increase your income, like a side business, as an excuse to save more money since you're making more money.

An emergency fund should be at least six months of your life's expenses. If you spend $1,000 a month on bills and expenses, then make sure your emergency fund has at least $6,000 in it. After hitting the six-month goal, you can keep saving or you can use the extra money to start investing.

So, set a goal and automate! Do whatever you have to do to save for emergencies because they do happen and they happen without notice.

Read more about automation on page 139.

Work on Your Cherished Relationships

There are some relationships in your life that you just can not live without even though these relationships can be difficult. We need to be with our loved ones and people who make us feel safe and supported. People to tun to when things go wrong. People who are reliable. People who are family (not necessarily blood relatives). Do your best to keep these people in your life and be sure to check up on them often.

If you have trouble with these people, see what happens if you bring yourself 100% into the relationship without expecting anything in return. Allow yourself to fully love these people and do your damnedest to work through the issues. Sometimes, your selfishness may be holding the relationship back.

Cherish these connections. Strive to create the family-bond. But, if the relationship is too toxic and you have done everything you can to try to mend it, maybe it's time to let some people go.

Let Go of Others

Letting go of people may be the most difficult thing we have to do. But if these people are bringing you down with negativity and are overall toxic to your life and mental well-being, it is time to cut ties and move on. You don't have to think about it as a forever decision.

Negative, toxic people are people with low self-esteem who are working on their own personal issues that they project and take out on others. Maybe somewhere down the line, they will be able to change themselves and try to open up the relationship with you again. If they have changed, you might be able to have that cherished relationship again.

A warning though. People who claim they have changed within a short period of time is often lying to you and to themselves. If they were truly toxic to your life you have to let them go for the long term. Or you will get stuck in a depressive cycle of wanting to keep them around then getting hurt then letting them go and forgiving them only to get hurt again.

Delegate Responsibilities

Responsibilities can be a lot to handle. If you're super stressed, try delegating tasks to other people. You may be the type of person who thinks, "if I want it done right, better do it myself," but taking on too much will lessen your quality of work and add unneeded stress.

Leo Babauta, from ZenHabits.com, says, "If a task needs to be done but is not one of your most important tasks, and it can be done by someone else, delegate it. Sometimes you can get rid of half your to-do list by finding others who can do the task as well or even better than you can."

Delegating leaves the tasks that are best suited for you. Then, you can work in a fast, effective and productive manner. When you focus on the stuff that you're good at, then you can tackle an entire to-do list in no time.

Try delegating at work or at home. Give chores to others. Hire a virtual assistant. Then use the leftover time and energy to help them back or for yourself.

Quit Commitments

Some commitments you take on just to help or please others. You may not like these commitments. They may take away from doing activities that you enjoy and help you grow. If you have commitments that are not adding benefits to your life, try to quit them as soon as you can. You don't want to be a promise breaker but you also don't want to be worn so thin on something you don't enjoy.

When you don't enjoy doing something you start to dread it and then you don't put in your best efforts because you'll be unmotivated in your work. It's best to keep unwanted commitments to a minimum and then have commitments that give you a sense of purpose and joy. It's okay to say no or decline to take on responsibilities. If you can, try delegating. Giving responsibilities to someone who will enjoy it more is the best way to go.

If you are going to quit any commitments, be sure to give plenty of notice and give your best effort beforehand. This will build your character and give you the happiness of a job well done.

Give Yourself a Disconnected Break

We have grown to be connected online 24/7. We sometimes forget the present moment, our surroundings or the nature around us. When we give ourselves a break from being online we can start to be in the present, notice the beauty in nature and of life and start feeling less stress or anxiety over missing an update or notification. Being glued to the internet and constantly consuming useless information day in and day out can have consequences on your life. You may be less productive, have an addiction and develop a shorter attention span.

Missing an update or a notification is not the end of the world and you must tell yourself that you do not have enough time in the world to see every single update. Ask yourself if you actually want to waste all that time in the first place? Do you want weeks of your life wasted to scrolling through pointless feeds or do you want those weeks to be productive and full of life?

Give yourself a disconnected break. Go a day without internet. Schedule in internet time in your day. See page 133 to see how to stay away from the internet.

Learn How to Set Goals

Now that you are gaining a lot of time and freedom, you may have decided to schedule time for yourself or focus on areas of your life you would like to improve. A way to improve ourselves is by setting goals. Goals give us something to look forward to and something to achieve.

But we often set goals and don't actually finish them or give up on them before they're even started. We tend to do this because the goal we set is overwhelming, too large for a short time frame and unreasonable.

To overcome this we can set SMART goals and then use self-discipline to help us pull through.

SMART is an acronym and it's a checklist. The acronym stands for **S**pecific, **M**easurable, **A**ttainable, **R**ealistic and **T**imely (a time-frame). To set achievable goals they must fit into this checklist. For example, a goal of "losing 70 pounds in a month" is not a SMART goal. Yes, it is specific, measurable and timely, but it is not attainable or realistic to lose so much weight in a short amount of time.

Likewise, a goal of "writing a book" is not a

SMART goal. It is attainable, measurable and realistic but it is not specific and timely. A better goal would be to "write a non-fiction book in 1 year (actual dates and deadlines help) by spending at least 1 hour a day writing and editing."

After setting up some smart goals, the next steps is to actually work on achieving them. This can be done through self-discipline. Plan out your goals and discipline yourself to follow through. If you plan to write for an hour every day then write for an hour every day.

Breaking down your goal into smaller steps can help a lot. For instance, writing a book could be broken down into research, outlining, writing chapter one, etc.

Breaking down a goal helps you break through plateaus because if you can check off an item off the to-do list, even if it's a small task, it will make you feel accomplished and motivated to do another task.

Sometimes the hardest thing about achieving goals is taking the first step. Breaking down a huge goal into small chunks can help you get started because a tiny task is a lot less scary than a huge task.

YOU'RE
DOING
GREAT

MINIMALIST STORY

Hayley Forster
@hellosimplejoy – Instagram & Facebook
@simplejoypin - Pinterest

From being a child, I was a perfectionist. I wanted to be the best at everything – not in a competitive way – I just wanted to be the best version of myself for my mother. You see, from birth, my mum was seriously ill. Normal living for me was her being in and out of hospitals with various ailments. I didn't see it as unusual but I knew I was different from my friends.

My coping mechanism was to become the 'perfect daughter'. I didn't want to add more stresses and strains into the family so I became a gold star student and a very well behaved little girl - Mummy's little star! I wanted to be the reason she was happy and her purpose for being.

But then the unthinkable happened.

My mother died.

I was 13.

Everything shifted. I was unexpectedly thrown into this very adult world against my will.

To others, it didn't come as a total surprise. But to me - it was a shock. To be ill was one thing, but to die? She had been in and out of hospital all my life but she always came back. I was told by her doctor that I would get my mum home for the upcoming festivities. I didn't. She died December 22, 1997, three days before Christmas. People kept pointing out how tragic it was that she died so young. Forty-six didn't seem that young to me.

Then.

The loss of mum at such a young age knocked me sideways. How on earth could this happen? You don't lose a parent now! You lose them when you are older after you're married and have children. They will go to your wedding. They will help you look after your first born.

You don't lose them at 13.

The only way I could see this not happening to me again was to ensure I had complete control over everything in my life. After all, if I could see everything around me and knew all the minute details, what could come at me unexpectedly?

Control = no unexpected events = Hayley's safe.

As time passed, my memories of my mum began to diminish. I started to forget what she looked like, what she smelt like, what she sounded like. I struggled to recall events in our life despite my family talking about them in depth. I couldn't remember and I felt like I was losing her completely. This was when my hoarding started. My way of maintaining memories was to keep everything. I had boxes and boxes of 'memories' - I saw these as the story of my life and I didn't want to be for gotten.

Fast forward through 15 years of hoarding and controlling, and in 2012, I had my first daughter. Initially, as every new parent does, I didn't change my lifestyle at all. I could maintain everything in life as it was pre-kids! Of course, I could!

Erm, no.

My controlling nature becomes impossible. My daughter dictated everything we did, and I couldn't predict what was going to happen. This was my worst nightmare! What was going to stop the inevitable disaster from happening? I fought so hard against it – I set routines, I wrote things down, I was super prepared for all eventualities. These still didn't work – I still wasn't in control. I was putting a huge amount of pressure on myself. I was so scared of what was going to happen that I didn't want to leave the house and when I did, I had panic attacks.

Then along came the crawling stage. One thing that crawling babies do not do well with? Clutter. My years of hoarding had resulted in me having papers and boxes galore all around the house. I had 'stuff' everywhere. She would pull out things I forgot I even had and I spent most of my day following her around and clearing up after her.

The two things that defined me and protected me from the world – hoarding and controlling – became impossible in my new life. I felt like everything I had built to protect me was coming crumbling down, so much so, I ended up with severe post-natal depression and anxiety. I hit rock bottom.

When I look back now, I realize that by trying to be the 'best mother' I was actually having the opposite effect. The stress I was putting myself under was immense. I was what I used to class as 'dropping the ball'. My usual standards were not being met.

But guess what? Nothing disastrous happened – the world didn't end!

I then slowly started to realize that being in control and 'letting go' of things in life was OK. I mean, don't get me wrong I fought hard against this realization but the more and more it happened, the more it sat well with me and I started to realize that by letting things go I became calmer and more content. I finally realized there was more to life than the chase of perfection and control.

It was then I decided that I need to scrape myself off the floor and make a change. Instead of running around chasing my tail, I stopped and slowed down.

I, slowly over time, eliminated 70% of my possessions and would only commit to having things in my life that aligned with my values. I highlighted everything that wasn't serving me or my family and got rid of them over time, whether it be physical items, time commitments, finances, negative emotions and even negative people. By focusing on less, life actually became more.

As I had less 'stuff' in my life, I was able to use my time to focus on the happiness of me and my family and what more could I want? With this extra space and calm in my life, my depression and anxiety lifted – I became a different person. I used to be an uptight, controlling perfectionist who would plan everything to a T. Now I am a relaxed, carefree woman who throws caution to the wind, goes with the flow and doesn't indeed care if everything in her life is perfect – as long as she feels happy and content and so does her family. The fact of the matter is, the things that I wanted most in my life - more time, less stress, more money, more energy, more contentment, more fun and memory making, was all on the other side of owning less.

This drastic shift in my life suddenly opened up my eyes to the fact that everyone has the same problems that I had – I just hadn't noticed it before as I was exactly the same! We are all victims of a modern-day epidemic. As I looked around, everyone had the same things in common – they are constantly feeling overwhelmed, feeling like a failure, and feeling as if they have lost their identity. Unfortunately, this is now becoming more common and is a social norm – running from one thing to the next and not being able to focus on what truly matters to us. It's all about more, more, more, we try to be everything to everyone – stay-at-home mums, loving and supportive wives, successful employees – but instead of success and accomplishment – we get exhaustion, guilt and overwhelm.

This is when I realized everything I had learned through my challenges needed to be shared & my life took another turn. I left my corporate career and set about educating people on my experiences. I help people feeling overwhelmed overcome their challenges, guide them to find their calm and how to feel happy and contented EVERY DAY. I do this by teaching minimalism and simple living. I for one, can't think of a better job than coaching people to turn their lives around, just like I did.

Maintain

Maintain and Improve

Now that we've have stopped the madness and learned how to get things in order, it's time to figure out how you're going to maintain your new lifestyle.

You have gotten rid of a bunch of physical items and you have cleared out your digital space and you've cut back on responsibilities and commitments. You have found more time for yourself and more time for the things that matter the most to you.

The next section of this book is going to teach you how to maintain and continue to improve your life. You're going to improve the way you use the internet, better your personal, mental and financial health and do feel-good activities such as volunteering and living environmentally friendly.

Buy Quality

You've heard the phrase quality over quantity. Many people forgo purchasing quality items because they can buy more cheaper items for less or for the same amount as the quality item. However, in the long run, they are wasting money and resources. Going for a cheaper item may look like a good decision money wise but the cheaper item is going to become damaged faster and become unusable sooner than if you would have bought the higher-quality item.

This goes for clothes, kitchen appliances, furniture, cars, houses, etc. Now not all things should be expensive to last a longtime. There are certainly deals to be found and 2nd-hand stores are filled with nice-quality items, but we are living in a consumerist world where making items that last a lifetime isn't really a good business model for companies who are looking for repeat business when their product breaks.

Going forward, when purchasing materials that you need, consider saving a little more money to buy a good quality item that will last you for a good while.

Buy Only What Serves You

On the topic of buying and purchasing items that you need, be sure to think about your purchases and buy only what is going to be used and loved. You don't want to end up back where you started. Think about how you felt about all the things you had before. Think about the new feelings of calmness, relief or any other feelings you've had since decluttering your life. Which set of feelings do you wish to have?

It's really easy to revert back to old habits or into old lifestyles. Make sure to keep yourself in check when out shopping.

With every purchase, ask yourself:
- Will I use this item?
- What is it's purpose?
- Is it a good-quality item?
- Will this serve me well?

Items should only be bought if it has a purpose and it is used regularly.

Gift Giving

Gifts are great, but they add to the clutter and sometimes you just don't use the items you've received. Or, you just don't like the items. That's okay. Gifts are about the thought. Someone thought about you and gave you a gift to show you love and compassion. Be thankful that you were in their thoughts and accept the gift.

This can also happen vise-versa. You may be giving other people gifts that are not used or wanted. Here are some ideas on how to give and receive gifts without wasting items:

For You

Be upfront with your family. Tell them that you love them and appreciate being on their minds. Ask them politely to think about giving gifts that align with your new lifestyle and explain to them why you chose to be a minimalist.

Ask for certain gifts. Per the suggestion above, you could ask to gift experiences rather it be a concert, a pass to a national park, a day trip with them or even a dinner date with just the two of you. The experiences could be for both of you or just you. You could ask for perishables. You may have a favorite chocolate you could ask for or if you're really into cooking you could ask for spices or rice/potatoes that would save you money at the grocery store. You could ask for time with them. You could ask for nothing at all.

For Them

Here are some things that you could gift to others:

- Gift an experience.
- Gift your time.
- Gift your help.
- Gift a handwritten letter.
- Gift something that they need.

Experience ideas

- Travel
- Spas
- Concerts

Perishable Ideas

- Cook them dinner.
- Bake cookies.

Be mindful and communicate openly. If they still insist, you can re-gift the item or donate it.

Keep Things With Purpose

Every single thing that you own needs to serve a purpose for you. It should check one of the following:

- It makes your life better.
- It makes your life easier.
- You truly love it.

You should only keep things with purpose. As you go throughout life, your needs will change and some items that once served you no longer will. If this happens, it's okay to give them a new home. Over time, if you don't keep things in check, you risk ending up with a lot of things you don't need and you may end up back at square one again.

Everything that is serving you now might not serve you later and you should be willing to let go when the time comes.

Go Through Physical and Digital Items Periodically

Digital

Maintenance requires you keep everything in check. The easiest area of your life to get messy and out of control is your digital space because once you close down a folder you cannot see the files even though they're still there. Out of sight = out of mind.

To combat this, go through files, photos and bookmarks periodically to keep everything tidy and in check. Schedule it like an appointment. Set aside an hour each month to keep the digital files in check.

Digital clutter can multiply quickly in this digital era. Another practice you can try to implement is to change your habits when dealing with your digital life. Don't take a million photos (like explained earlier in this book), don't bookmark every single thing you find, don't sign up for a million newsletters you won't read and don't download items unless you're going to use them.

Physical

The same with your physical items. Over time, your situation changes and your lifestyle changes. Due to this, you may not need items that you still have and you may need items that you don't currently own. For this reason, you should go through your physical items periodically as well.

Get rid of everything you don't need and bring in things that you do need. Schedule an appointment to reassess or you may find that things will end up the way it was before your journey. Clutter has sneaky tendencies that slowly creep up on you without you noticing.

You need to nip it in the bud before you have to start all over. Don't get stressed out over stuff again. Keep it minimal.

Use The Internet Strategically

The internet fills a lot of needs and it's amazing. Entertainment, education, communication, tools and resources make up the internet and allow us to live advanced lives that we lead today. But with all this information, it's impossible to consume everything all the time especially if we want to maintain a good quality of life and not just lie around all day consuming information and scrolling through feeds.

For this, you need a strategy on how you are to use the internet. If you just want pure entertainment with social media, gossip sites and games, then make a plan on how to do just that and also maintain a good life outside the WiFi hotspot.

If you want to use tools and resources to improve your productivity and also learn new skills, you will also need a plan in place so you're not distracted by the entertainment side of things.

A way you can come up with a strategy is scheduling in internet time. you can schedule when you're going to learn, when to check email or social media and when to relax and play games.

Follow People That Inspire Not Spam

Instead of following everyone on social media like people who seem cool or family and friends try to follow people that inspire you to achieve the goals you want to achieve. There are awesome people achieving your goals and by following them you could get insight on how to achieve it yourself and get inspiration to follow through.

A lot of our feeds are cluttered because we like and follow every single account that seems interesting. Or we just follow people we vaguely know to spy into their lives and be nosy. Admit it!

But, all those accounts distract you from your goals. They may make you sad or angry and emit negative emotions based on the content. If you follow inspiring accounts, they may put a pep in your step and get you motivated to get productive!

Clear up your feed and turn it into a positive, inspiring and motivating place to scroll through. If your feed is cluttered to the max, you may want to check out my social media challenge on page 94 to declutter your feeds for good.

Get Health Checks

It's easy knowing that we should regularly see a doctor, but a lot of people don't go unless they have a serious ailment or injury. It's a good idea to see the doctor every two years, if not every year, to see if your health is improving or declining. This is good so you know if you need to change anything health or exercise wise before it's too late.

Sometimes making an appointment is scary especially if you know something is wrong because of neglect on your part.

For example, I stopped having a good oral hygiene practice for about a year. Then I felt shame, guilt and fear when I examined my mouth to see cavities and severely discolored teeth.

I knew this would happen if I didn't brush twice a day and floss. So, I was terrified of making a dentist appoint for fear of judgment and if the problem was not reversible.

Life happens, but you need to suck up your pride and get checked out before it's too late.

Exercise Consistently

Exercising is essential for our well-being, for both fitness and mental health. Exercising consistently will help you keep to the schedule and not jump off the bandwagon. Commit to exercising no less than 3 times a week and try to get small daily movements in every day even if it's a 30-minute walk.

Optimally, forty minutes of vigorous or ninety minutes of low-intensity exercising a day is recommended by doctors. So shooting for this number most days should be a goal to strive towards, but starting out small is the way to go to get your body adjusted and without burning out.

Some ways to make sure you're meeting your goals:

- Get an accountability partner.
- Get an exercise buddy.
- Join a workout bet.
- Put money on the line on stickk.com.
- Sign up and commit to workout classes.

Have a Sleep Routine

Sleep is important for our health and getting 7-9 hours a night is optimal. Not only should you shoot for the required hours, but you try to establish a routine for when you go to bed and when you wake up. Being consistent with waking up and sleeping will help your body function better and know when it needs to settle down and when it needs to get active.

You don't want to feel tired when you should have plenty of energy and you don't want to be hyper when you want to sleep. Inconsistent sleep patterns will mess up your energy cycles.

It doesn't matter what your routine is as long as you're consistent about it. If you're a night owl and have loads of energy later in the evening, make your schedule, routine and commitments around that. Like-wise for morning birds.

If life commitments have final say on when you should sleep or rise, then make sure you are getting plenty of sleep and make sure you are consistent. Your body will eventually adapt to the new schedule. Help it out by getting plenty of sleep.

Whole Foods Will Do You Good

Plant-based foods are Nature's miracle foods. They always say to eat your fruits and vegetables and for good reason too. Plant foods give your body all the vitamins and minerals it craves and it's packaged in low calories which means you can eat as much as you want and not feel deprived.

Reading books like How Not to Die, Eat to Live, The Starch Solution and Forks Over Knives will give you more insight on why plant foods, and a primarily plant-based diet, is superior and beneficial to one's health and well being.

Plus, plant-based foods are the ultimate minimalist foods. They're quick, easy, not complicated, impactful, healthy, environmentally-friendly and taste good with less preparation. Most plant foods can be eaten raw so literally, no effort is needed to eat them.

If you don't want to waste time cooking and cleaning up, or if you want to simplify your diet to be as healthy as you can, consider adding more plant foods in your life. Anything yummy goes such as fruits, vegetables, tubers, legumes, whole grains, nuts and seeds.

Automate Finances

Automating finances improves your finances because you won't have to do a whole lot of work when everything is taken care of for you. When things are on autopilot according to your financial plans, it's easier to stick to your plans and get ahead in your goals because there's no room for cheating.

If money is automatically scheduled to withdraw from your bank and deposit into a savings account, then you will more than likely achieve your goals. When you have to personally withdraw and deposit, you are more prone to NOT doing it because you'll tell yourself that you can "do it later" or you "can't save this pay" because you want to go shopping.

Setting up automation will make you achieve your goals without any effort. Here are some ways you can automate:

- Automatic savings each payday
- Automatic investments every month
- Automatic bill pay
- Automatic debt repayment

Add Multiple Streams of Income

Multiple streams of income (MSI) are very important for financial independence. It helps you become more stable in the event of one stream of revenue ending with a layoff or resignation. They say you should look for a steady job that brings you stable income. That's cool and all, but it's not so stable when you randomly get laid off.

Then you're screwed because you have no money coming in and you have mouths to feed and bills to pay. Having one, steady job is not stable. I'll repeat this. Having a steady job, even if it's full-time with benefits, is not stable if it's your only income.

You should have multiple sources of income to create a steady and STABLE flow of money. If one stream goes down, you won't be completely screwed over and struggling to find another job because you will have other sources to hold you afloat, so you can job search without panicking.

Having income coming in on the side lets you contribute more towards your financial goals as well. Your main job can be for main bills and your side gig can be used for destroying debt, vacation money, emergency money, investment money or just fun money.

MSI Ideas

- Start a side business such as an online store, online tutoring, or blogging.
- Create an information product like a book, an online education course, or an informational blog.
- Learn to code and create a bootstrapped startup.
- Freelance your skills like website development, writing, graphic design or virtual assisting.
- Etc.

There are a million ways to get extra income online and plenty of ways to make extra income offline. Use your skills, research and get hustling.

Meet Like-Minded People

Finding people who share the same hobbies, goals and interests with you will help you reach your best potential.

You can find people to build you up and become your supporters in life. It helps to find people who are living your goals and values. They say you will become like the five people you mostly hang around. Make sure those five people are succeeding in life and are good people, so you can be motivated to make strides in your own life.

You can find peers online through meetup.com. There you search local groups of people with the same interests as you.

Only hang with people that you like, that inspire you and that don't bring you down. You want to be encouraged not discouraged.

*Bonus points if these people are also minimalists :)

Check Up On Your Loved Ones

In the busyness of life, it's sometimes easy to gloss over the most important parts. Your loved ones and the people who are closest to you should be a main priority in your life after yourself.

Sooner or later these people are going to get older and if they leave this world before you, you don't want to regret not spending more time with them.

So, write those letters, makes those calls, schedule those visits. Most importantly make sure to voice your love and give hugs.

Do Things With Purpose

Volunteer

Charitable actions don't only win karma points, but it lets you help others selflessly which will boost your spirits because you will feel good for doing good. Giving without expecting anything in return is a beautiful, heart-warming experience that makes you feel more connected to a cause.

Some ways to find opportunities:

- Libraries
- Schools
- Zoos and Museums
- Animal Shelters
- Websites:
    - www.volunteermatch.org
    - www.dosomething.org
    - www.volunteer.gov

Now, you can also give to charity by exercising! Go to www.charitymiles.org to download the app. Then, give to charity every mile you walk, run or bike.

Use your skills to volunteer

You can volunteer to use your skills to help out charities and non-profit organizations. If you have a specific skill such as website development, photography, graphic design, baking, etc., you can be very valuable to an organization in need.

Charities don't have a big budget, but they need things such as a website or marketing to spread their message. You can do them a huge favor while also boosting your own resume with related experience.

If your skill if what you do for a living then having extra experience is a plus when job searching. This will show employers that you are so passionate about your field of work that you will help others with your skills.

For example, if you know how to build websites, you can take that skill and volunteer to make or redo the websites of charities such as animal shelters. In doing so, you can get more experience, have a website for your portfolio of work and do good at the same time.

Be Environmentally Friendly

By being a minimalist and living a lifestyle of less you may notice that it can go hand-in-hand with being environmentally friendly. For one, just owning less and consuming less will reduce your footprint. By cleaning up your diet you'll lower your footprint and if you start buying high-quality items that last a long time, you'll, again, lower your footprint.

Being environmentally friendly lets you enjoy your life while also lessening the damage to the Earth. We should all do our parts to ensure the Earth will stick around for our grandchildren.

Here are some ways to be environmentally friendly:

- Go Vegan!
- Make your own food from scratch. (Local and in--season ingredients are bonus points)
- Wash clothes in cold water only
- Stop using and buying plastic water bottles and use reusable ones instead
- Turn off the lights when leaving the room

More ways to go green can be found on: greenasathistle.com.

Make Time For Personal Growth

Make time for yourself. Not only should you make time to rest and relax, but make time to grow. Working to grow and geting better makes sure you are consistently improving your life instead of staying in the same place. Make time to explore yourself. Learn a new skill, read thought-provoking books, start and strive for big goals and be one with yourself. Also, make sure to love yourself or learn to love yourself. Loving and accepting yourself and your body will give you the strength to achieve anything.

Schedule this time for yourself. Make an appointment with yourself as if it's an important business meeting. You should be your number one priority. Take care of yourself and your life then you can help others.

***

I hope you enjoyed this book. This book has been my secret love for over two years. I wrote this book to help myself out and to have something to reference when I get stuck in my life. I hope this helps you as well. I hope your life gets better, and I hope you pass this book along when you no longer have a use for it.

Appendix

This appendix is filled with extras and tips that didn't fit in the rest of the book. Simply Minimal was all about YOU and YOUR needs. It didn't touch on your spouse, kids or other areas such as traveling.

I've done my best to give you all the knowledge that I have. If you are looking for something else, visit the companion website at simplyminimal.life to find other voices that can help you out. For example, I don't have any children so my advice in this department is not so feasible, but on the website, I have looked over the web at the best minimalist parenting advice there is and I have listed them here for you.

Appendix Contents:

Living Arrangements

Kids

Spouses

Travel

Why I Didn't Bother Selling My Things

A Minimalist Wedding

Why I Love the Library

Why I Bike to Work

5 Minutes of Stress Relief

Being Eco-Friendly and Sustainable

living arrangements

Your living arrangements can have a big impact on your minimalist journey. Having a bigger home than what you need, tends to feel empty after downsizing everything. You may learn that you are able to live in a smaller place that you thought. Although, having a lot of empty space can be relaxing, having too much might make you want to start filling up the place again. You don't want that!

Owning a House

Moving into a smaller space can have many benefits. You can save a lot of money. If you are renting, it's cheaper to live in a smaller house or unit. If you are a homeowner, living in a smaller house can reduce your mortgage.

And since we're on the topic of mortgages, try to steer clear of mortgages as much as possible. A house is not truly yours if you have a mortgage. It's the bank's. Mortgages are a life sentence like student loans. So, save save save until you can buy a home outright, or save save save so you can have a HUGE down payment, so you can get a smaller mortgage and a shorter loan period.

If you already have a mortgage, or if a mortgage is the best option for you, consider paying it down as quick as possible. See page 102 for how to pay down debts.

Other than houses, there are different living arrangements that you can consider that may compliment your new minimalist lifestyle.

Mobile Homes Are Great

Many people look over trailers because of the idea that living in a trailer park is dangerous, drug-infested and low-class. However, this might be a money-saving goldmine. A lot of trailer parks are nice, high-quality and quiet. You have to do your homework and go check out the places. But, you might be surprised to find that some parks look beautiful and like actual suburban neighborhoods.

Mobile homes are also cheap to buy. Although some run as much as a small house, you can easily find decent homes that cost between 5-20 thousand dollars. Then, you need to worry about the ground rent at the park that is way below any house or apartment rental.

You can even park them on your own land and skip paying the ground rent all together! You should look into mobile homes! They were the original tiny homes!

Unconventional Living

Some other places that people have found themselves living by choice are vehicles. Cars, RVs, campers, vans and converted buses are all different places that people call home. This method gives people the freedom to live anyplace they can travel to.

Although this style may be too small for most people or too scary, if you're interested in looking into it, it may be the thing you are looking for.

Another unconditional living arrangement is nomadic living. Nomads have no home (intentionally) and travel all over. They sleep in hotels, hostels, tents etc. They call the world their home and they go where they please and are not held down by an address.

The internet today, has given a lot of people the option of being a nomad. They can work anywhere in the world on a computer to make money and then travel as they please. Pretty interesting!

kids

I honestly have no advice for children since I don't have any. But, being an older sister of 11 munchkins, I have observed a few things:

- Kids have a lot of toys and they only play with 20% of them.
- Kids these days don't go outside enough because they are glued to screens.
- Kids are willing to give up lesser-liked toys for a good cause.

More advice from actual parents on simplyminimal.life/kids

spouses

My husband has more clothes than me and that's okay. The first time he said, "I need to go through my clothes and get rid of some," sparked so much joy in me that I almost wept. His things and clothes and tools are a major stress in my life. It's so much that's not being used!

But a lot of people don't get the get-rid-of-your-things-and-you'll-be-happier thing. I didn't get it back then either! I had to be "enlightened, " and he does too.

So, lead the way and eventually, your spouse will start seeing all your gains, you with less stress and will want to join in. You can show them how much easier life is when you don't have to drag around so much stuff.

Accept Them

But, sometimes it takes a long time or it might not work at all. And it that case you have to accept them as a person and love them for who they are. If you truly love them you will have to overlook many things. I'm sure there are other things about them that you accept out of love and there are things about you that they accept. Because love is the love of who they are.

travel

Traveling gets super easy as a minimalist. You will only pack the essentials leaving you with lighter luggage, fewer things to haul and carry, and less money spent on luggage checks and souvenirs.

Here are some packing tips:

- Cut down on luggage by reducing your items to what can fit in a book bag. This forces you to only carry the essentials.
- Get a book bag that can be considered a carry-on at most airlines and make sure it has lots of compartments for organization.
- Get packing cubes to fit in your book bag to hold clothes in a compact way.
- Roll up your clothes to save space and make them stackable.

The Clothes Trick

My clothes trick for traveling saves space and reduces the number of clothes you need to bring. Count the number of days you will be gone then cut it in half. You will then pack that many outfits.

So, if you're on a 10-day trip, only bring enough clothes for 5 days. The trick is to wear the outfits twice before presuming them dirty. If you're gone more than 10 days, see if you can get access to laundry. That will help you reduce your load in your book bag to save space and to bring fewer clothes.

why i didn't bother selling my things

/ This was a blog post originally published on
GreenAsAThistle.com. /

It has been more than a year since I have embraced minimalism and gotten rid of so many things that I thought I would keep forever. During that time when I was devouring every blog post, I could find on minimalism. I read different ways people dealt with their clutter. Most recommended to sort through the clutter and to separate it into three piles: sell, donate and trash. People wanted to get some money back on items they spent so much money on. I, however, didn't spend anything on my items. I was 19 years old, in college and broke.

Most of my items came from Goodwill or have been handed down to me by different family members. That means I could just sell my items for profit, no? Well, here are some reasons why I didn't bother selling my things.

Too Much Hassle

From taking pictures of each and every item to making separate posts for each item is a real pain. Not to mention the hassle of signing up for a site, inputting your information, dealing with the customers and then shipping the items. Too much work for very little payback if you ask me. It is way too much time consuming, and it is so much easier to just put everything into a box and ship it to Goodwill.

I Rather Give To People In Need

I grew up in poverty with a single mother. We always had our basic needs met, but we just couldn't afford to go out shopping at the big outlets. So, every other week we would end up at Goodwill. It was our favorite place, besides the Dollar Tree. Being that we always had others helping us, I wanted to freely give my things to people who needed them free of charge.

I'm Lazy

I am so lazy. I never wanted to put in the effort to even think about selling things. I just wanted everything to be gone as soon as I decided I didn't need it anymore. Seeing my room become clearer and clearer gave me more momentum to get rid of more things.

That is why I didn't sell any of my things. Besides being too lazy to do so, it would have been a giant hassle especially when I was dealing with college and an internship and finding a job and life! It's great if you want to put in the time to get back some of what you paid for things, and I definitely recommend selling textbooks. But, for me, I just wanted to be done with the clutter.

a minimalist wedding

/ This was a blog post originally published on
GreenAsAThistle.com. /

I'm getting married in February! And, aside from keeping the costs minimal, I'm trying to have a minimalist wedding. What does that mean? Well, minimalism is keeping and doing only what you need and what you absolutely care about.

So, technically, a minimalist wedding would be getting married in a courthouse with two witnesses, a couple of rings and a kiss. If that's your wedding, great! You've saved time, money, stress and commotion. But, for me to get married, I want to have my family around me. I want to have a ceremony and a reception. These things will be giving me plenty of joy.

What I don't need, however, is a big, extravagant celebration that is going to leave me regretful when we need to buy a new car or if a medical emergency pops up. Money is a big issue, and it's great to know that just by sticking to minimalism, I can automatically reduce my costs.

161

No Gifts

We've already sent out our invitations stating that we do not want gifts. We've listed a couple charities and said that we would also appreciate chocolate and money. Consumables. My goal is to move into an RV and I can't do that if the whole family wants to buy us dishes, vacuums, microwaves and towel sets. I'm getting anxiety just thinking about it.

Small Venue

We knew that we wanted a small wedding. Close family and a couple friends would be more than enough to celebrate our day. We didn't know that 50 people would be our max. Our venue is so small that they restricted us to 50 people. Which is great because that's just what we need. I was filling out a guest list and I found myself including friends that I haven't spoken to or seen in person in 5 years. The limit really helped us nip it in the bud on the people that truly matter to our lives.

Buffet

We refuse to spend a fortune on catering ($80

a head SERIOUSLY?!?). Why spend money when I have a family wanting to help out? So, we're having a basic dessert table and a buffet of soup, tacos and salads. We're also having a setup for coffee, tea and hot chocolate because it is going to be February. This lets everyone have the freedom of getting what they want and minimizes planning on my end.

Decorations

My fiancé and I are not the ones to care about decorations or if something looks nice. We only care about the item's functioning use. So, with help of my mom, we are going to have minimal decorations. Basic table liners, bows on the backs of chairs and my mom rocks at staging food.

Bride's Beauty

I am not the one who cares about beauty. I never wore makeup, I never put any product except for shampoo and conditioner in my hair, I never owned a straightener or curling iron and I don't know what contouring is. The only thing I do is paint my nails (white, always white) and wear rings and earrings. I never found this necessary.

But, bride's are supposed to do all this right? It's a day of glitz and glam. Well, not for me. I will not be wearing makeup, heels or getting my hair professionally done. I'm keeping my natural look with a simple french braid and painted white nails. It fits the theme of my wedding which is the love garden (since it's Valentine's Day and we're getting married in a greenhouse).

So, these are some things that I'm doing to keep my wedding minimal. I see a lot of weddings that are beautiful and extravagant. But, I can't believe that they did all this work, spent all this money, for one day of celebrating. I believe we can have a magical day without going over-the-top.

why i love the library

/ This was a blog post originally published on
GreenAsAThistle.com. /

I admit that I have a collection. As a minimalist, that is frowned upon, but I don't care! This collection is really near and dear to me. It represents all the places I have lived. An interesting fact about me is that I am 21 years old, and I have had 16 different addresses. Needless to say, my family moves around a lot. New places, neighbors, scenery and schools were a given. But, libraries were always a constant. They were always there.

So my collection? Library cards. I have every library card I have ever had. They mean a lot to me. It represents two things that I love: books and memories of places. I don't have 16 different library cards because I lived in several different addresses in the same library district, but they each represent a different time period in my life.

I still go to the library. I think I go at least once a week. Especially nowadays since I read so much. And, I have noticed that all the libraries I have gone to have the same theme: renting resources. Libraries are true minimalists. They are a hub of resources that they share freely with the public. And, the resources are not just books.

Books

Starting with books, these are what automatically comes to mind when someone mentions the word "library." They have a great thing going on. Instead of spending hundreds of dollars a month to read all the books I want, I can check it out from the library for free. It's really great to return the book when I'm done without it adding to my clutter.

I also like it when a library has a holding system. I love browsing for books on the online catalog and requesting them online even if that book is currently across town at a different library I normally don't go to. I can request it, and the library ships the books to the branch I want to go to. Talk about service.

Another thing I love about my library is inter-library loans. If my library system doesn't have a book I want, I can request an inter-library loan. I give a librarian the details of the book I'm after and she'll contact ALL the libraries in the state that are partnered up and get the book for me. This option sometimes comes with a price, but I haven't had to pay anything the two times I've used it.

One more thing regarding books is that you can often suggest a library to buy a book they don't have. If they feel, the book is popular enough, they'll buy it and let you know when they have it in stock.

Entertainment

I don't use this feature, but many libraries rent out CDs and DVDs. Their selection isn't as big as their book selection, but a quick browse through shows all the popular TV shows people talk about, so it's worth checking out.

Databases

Libraries partner with online services that usually charge a hefty penny. But, by using it through the library it is free. If you're researching a topic that doesn't have sufficient information in books, I suggest seeing what type of databases your library has.

Rooms

A lot of libraries have private rooms for patrons to go in and read/work away from the main area. It can offer peace and quiet. These rooms are often big enough for several people to occupy, but with an absolute no sounds rule, you won't even notice the other people.

Libraries also have conference rooms that have to be reserved in advance. And sometimes, they're limited to businesses and non-profit groups. But, if anyone can reserve a room, it might be worth checking out the next time you have a group project. These rooms come with whiteboards and plenty of tables.

Also, in the main library area, there are PLENTY of quiet spaces and sitting areas. There are some corners that offer super comfy chairs, a section for teens to hang out, private seating by some windows, etc. I love going in, grabbing a seat and enjoying the view. The main area isn't too loud unless you're near the kid/teen zone and even then, the noise is minimal.

Activities

Many libraries host a number of activities in the library. They teach classes, offer story-time, host book clubs and invite speakers and workshops to teach a skill or share a resource. There are plenty of things to do. I even saw a yoga class on the calendar. Libraries are part of the community and they bring people together. Classes may or may not be free. Most of them require that you sign up in advance.

WiFi

Wonderful, free WiFi. I often see many people blogging/tweeting/instagramming about working in coffee shops. But, coffee shops are loud and promote spending money on yummy, unhealthy, sugary goodness. I never see people share that they're working from a library. I wonder why?

Tech Equipment

Some libraries have equipment you can use. There may be a section of computers that have Adobe products on them, they may have digital cameras you can work with and some teen sections have video games. All fun.

And, all the libraries I have been to have computers that the public can use.

Libraries are an amazing place and it's a shame that people associate them with being boring. I love the library and will continue to use their resources.

why i bike to work

/ This was a blog post originally published on
GreenAsAThistle.com. /

I've been commuting to work by bike for about a year now (minus 3 months when the area decided to freeze over for winter). At first, it was my only option. I was fresh out of college with my very first job in my field of study. I had no license. I still lived at home but with my single mother's busy and hectic schedule, I didn't want to bother adding another two stops to her day. I also wanted to show independence. I was sick of relying on unreliable people, so I decided I would start biking to work.

At first, it was a challenge. All I had was my old mountain bike that had no breaks. I had this bike for about 7 years. It had been my 'horse,' 'motorcycle' and any other imaginative thing a preteen could come up with. It was out of shape. But, there was a bike shop on the commute, so I would stop there to get it fixed up on my ride home.

Another challenge was that the commute was 5 miles. That's one way. So, that was 10 miles a day. For being very overweight and out of shape at the time, very didn't mix so well with the bike being in bad condition. So, I rode 5 miles to work in the early morning heat on a bike with no breaks in hilly Pittsburgh. I had to stop half way through to take a break and drink water. I had to walk my bike down hills. My knees were killing me.

On the way home I stopped at the bike shop. They did the best they could, but they told me that the gearbox is in bad shape and it would only stay in one gear. At least I had breaks.

I continued on with the week. By the end of it, my butt was extremely sore, my knees were killing me and I had two flat tires to deal with it, but I knew this thing was a thing I wanted to do. So, I started researching about biking and commuting. I knew with my first paycheck, I would treat my family to dinner, but I would also buy a new bike.

This time, it wouldn't be a mountain bike. I had learned that their tires are not good on leveled, smooth land. There's too much friction and that would make you go slower. That explains why it would take me 45 minutes to do 5 miles. I also saw many others on bikes that had skinny tires and you had to lean forward. They were going pretty fast, but they looked weird (the riders looked weird, too), and I was scared that the skinny tires would always get flats.

So, I looked at hybrid bikes and got one. It cut 15 minutes off of my commute and I tweeted many times that it was the best ride I had ever felt. 10 miles a day? Bring it on.

Later that year, my fiance and I moved to an apartment closer to my work. So 10 miles a day has been cut down to 3 miles a day. Sometimes, I miss the longer commute. But either way, I love biking to work and here's why:

- **It's freedom.** I still don't have a driver's license and this is a way I can have a taste of mobility freedom.

- **It's different.** Although I see many people commuting by bike, I still feel like we're going against the norm. The majority of people drive, walk or take public transportation. It feels good to be different and it's a great conversation starter.

- **It saves money.** Living and working in a city, you have to pay to park which is extremely expensive. Just having a car is expensive. And, also, I'm not wasting any gas.
- **It's faster than a car.** Don't believe me? Let's have a race in a city with city traffic.
- **It sneaks in exercise.** It's an excellent exercise. I believe biking 10 miles a day really jump-started my 40lb weight loss to date.
- **It's nice to be exposed to fresh air.** Everyone these days seems to be stuck indoors. But, it's nice to have some fresh air every day.

5 minutes of stress relief

/ This was a blog post originally published on
GreenAsAThistle.com. /

Since we all have lives, there's comes a time where we feel really stressed out. This may be once in a while or it may be often, but stress can have negative effects on our body. It is a sign that we are feeling overwhelmed and that we need to have a break.

But, how can you possibly have a break when you have so much to do, and you have no time? Well, breaks don't have to mean a half hour lunch break or an hour relaxing in a bath. We can treat ourselves to 5-minute mini-breaks that will take our stress levels down and leave us feeling re-freshed. Here's a list you can do if you're feeling stressed and need to relax.

Listen to Your Favorite Song (or Two). Sit back, close your eyes and don't do anything else but listen to the song. If you are afraid of people distracting you, you can always go into a bathroom stall. Another thing you could do is dance to the music if you're feeling a little energetic.

Meditate with Calm

Calm.com is a great website that has wonder-ful, natural sounds that will calm you. It even has an option to guide you through meditation with simple prompts on the screen. They also have an app, so you can 'calm' wherever you are.
Stretch

Get up and stretch! Your body is sore from running around. Take a few minutes to stretch out your muscles, so they can keep working for you.

Take a Walk

Make it a power walk, so you can get the blood flowing. Spend 5 minutes walking up and down stairs, around your building or outside.

Take in Nature

Take a moment to admire nature. Your days can go by so fast that you forget what a beautiful thing our planet is. So, take in a sunset, a garden, a body of water, wild animals and even man-made art and architectures

Our days are stressful, but it doesn't have to be if we regularly give our bodies a break during the day. Try out some of these tips and see the calming results afterward.

being eco-friendly, less wasteful and sustainable

/ This was a blog post originally published on GreenAsAThistle.com. /

Over the years I have radically reduced by possessions, consumption and waste. I have been interested in being green and saving the environment since I was 14 years old. I use to make information packets to pass along to my family to get them to recycle. I read books on how to be green, making natural products and reducing my carbon footprint for fun. This topic is very important to me.

Since then, I have grown to be very environmentally conscious. People and businesses are waking up and changing. Products are being made from recycled material and are energy-efficient and businesses are striving to be sustainable. These are all good things, but we can do better.

sustainability isn't enough

sus·tain·a·ble

adjective

1. able to be maintained at a certain rate or level.

The above definition says that to be sustainable is to maintain a certain rate or level. In terms of the environment, people and businesses are looking into sustainability to maintain their level of consumption while not damaging the planet any further. However, being sustainable isn't enough to save the Earth. We need to change our lifestyles for the better. Of course, this is something that people hate to do.

People know that they are being wasteful just like they know they are making a poor health choice when eating fried foods. But, they don't care. They rather take medications to cover up their ailments due to the poor lifestyle choices instead of actually changing said lifestyle choices. And they rather keep living and consuming the way they are and just cover everything up by being sustainable.

How can you live exactly the same while not damaging the planet? You can't. If everyone on Earth lived the same as the average American consumer, we would need 4 extra Earths to live and survive. I'm sorry to say that we only have one planet and we need to strive for more than just sustainability.

Let's take disposable, plastic water bottles as an example. Sustainability says we can keep this habit if we recycle the bottle and purchase bottles that are made from recycled plastic. That's good, but making the plastic in the first place caused damage to the Earth. A better solution is to not buy disposable water bottles and use reusable bottles instead.

We should focus on not being wasteful, reducing our carbon-footprint and changing our lifestyles for the better. Stop trying to live the same life and expect better results from the planet. If you want different results, you have to be different.

minimalism can help

Minimalism is the practice of getting rid of everything in your life that is not serving a purpose, that is not useful to you or that doesn't bring you joy. Minimalists keep only the important things in their lives and let go of the rest. At first, minimalism is about getting rid of things (and hopefully these things are given new life and are not ending up in landfills), but then it becomes about being conscience on what you bring into your life.

Minimalists are known to consume less and care about how items were made. By accepting minimal, high-quality items that last a long time into their lives, minimalists reduce their carbon footprints. Less stuff means less waste.

Not all minimalists think about their impact on the environment, but just by bringing fewer things into your life can have a positive impact towards greening up the Earth.

ways that i am green

Here are the areas in my life that I have reduced. I make most of my own products, stopped doing "normal" hygiene regimens and some things, like shaving my legs, have never interested me in the first place.

Bathroom

Shampoo – I like to use natural shampoo such as Güd shampoo, but I've been experimenting with water only washing.

Conditioner – I haven't used conditioner in 2

years. No, my hair isn't dried out.

No Shaving – Never liked it, so I completely stopped shaving. I don't own a razor!! Sometimes (about once a month), I do trim my legs with my husband's beard clippers and I do use an epilator on my armpits.

Toothpaste – I used to make my own toothpaste, but now, I just brush my teeth using water. Once a week or so, I'll brush with baking soda.

Face Wash – I used to to the oil-cleansing method, now I just wash my face with water and a cloth (I may go back to oil-cleansing).

Kitchen

Diet – I have been vegetarian since 2011 and I recently became a vegan.

Making Food – I make 97% of my food myself with all natural ingredients.

Laundry

Detergent – I have been using Eco-Nuts since 2015.

Cold Water – I always wash all my clothes in the cold-water setting.

Disposables

Ban the Bottle – I sometimes call myself a reusable water-bottle snob. I prefer glass. I like at least 32oz. Since my beloved glass bottle broke last summer, I've been searching for a replacement. But, I've been using a mason jar and it's been working out great. I don't drink water from plastic bottles.

Toxins

No Perfume – I was never interested in wearing perfumes, but once in a blue moon, I would use some. Now, I have none.

Air Freshener – I've been making my own air freshener with essential oils. 15 drops of Lavender Oil into a spray bottle. Fill with water, shake and spray.

areas for improvement

Paper Towels – I've been using a lot of paper towels lately. Every time I go to the bathroom and wash my hands I use a piece to dry off. It's a habit that needs to go.

Packaging – As I'm shopping, I don't care to think about how much packaging an item has before buying it. You should try to go with items that have less packaging.

Plastic Bags – During checkout, I never bring a reusable shopping bag, so I consume shopping bags. I used to make excuses as to why this was okay.

Soap – I'm starting to take notice of the chemicals in soaps.

Electricity – I used to keep everything unplugged when things weren't in use, now everything is plugged in all the time.

I plan to improve the above over time. I want to treat every day as if it's Earth Day. I will pause to think before consuming. I will air dry my hands, steal a reusable tote bag from my mom to go grocery shopping, avoid over-packaged stuff and buy natural soaps. As for electricity, I will flick the switches when the husband leaves.

how you can become green

Changing habits take time. But, you can definitely look at your life and change to do your part for the environment. Consume less, eat more naturally and locally, volunteer and plant a couple of trees. And for the environment's sake, please don't try to be sustainable. Actually, change. Here a list of easy things to get started today:

Never buy paper towels again. You will get creative when you make messes like using hand towels.

Never buy paper/styrofoam/plastic dishes again. Don't be lazy. Actually, wash the dishes instead of filling up landfills.

- Cook at home and from scratch more often.
- Get a water filter and a reusable bottle.
- Eat way less meat.
- Revamp your hygiene with natural, green products.
- Volunteer to plant a tree.

books and resources I recommend

Calculators

www.nature.org/greenliving/carboncalculator/

www.carbonfootprint.com/calculator.aspx

carbonfootprint.c2es.org

Books

Sleeping Naked is Green – Vanessa Farquharson

Wearing Smaller Shoes: Living Light on the Big Blue Marble – Chip Haynes

No Impact Man – Colin Beavin

The Zero-Waste Lifestyle: Live Well by Throwing Away Less – Amy Korst

Going Green for Dummies

Documentaries

An Inconvenient Truth

Cowspiracy

No Impact Man

Blogs

Here's 100 of them:

www.environmentalsciencedegree.com/green-living/

Charities

The National Conservancy

Wildlife Conservation Network

That is all for now. Please be kind.

I would like to thank
- Brandon, my husband
- Mamie
- Pop
- Mom and her DimWitts
- The James Gang
- Teah
- Frappe
- Cookies
- Ice
- Rumple

for being there for me, supporting me and helping me stay sane while I finally finished this book.

I would like to thank the internet for always being my inspiration to everything I do.

Thank you all so much! I love you.

<3 KT

ABOUT THE AUTHOR

Hey! I'm Katelyn Cresmer ,or KT on the internet. I help people simplify all areas of life to be healthy, financially fit and successful. On GreenAsAThistle.com, I write about minimalism, living eco-friendly, eating plant-based and how living like this can create a life of freedom and financial Independence.

Other than that, I am a hippie without the trippie, professional watermelon eater and a stay-at-home catmom with a bun.

JOIN ME!

Over at Green as a Thistle, I document my journey into minimalism! I have my life hacks and tips that have worked for me over the years to transform my life.

Join the newsletter and get access to updates, a free 7-day decluttering course, a discount code for the ebook, 1-on-1 conversations with me and access to amazing resources to help you with your journey.

Sign up today: **greenasathistle.com/hello**

CHRISTEAH

The only self-publishing service that makes sure your book has the most chance of success WITHOUT profiting off of your book.

We never take a penny from your book sales. Your royalties are yours.

Join the waitlist: **christeah.press**

www.ingramcontent.com/pod-product-compliance
Lightning Source LLC
LaVergne TN
LVHW051511080426
835509LV00017B/2025